DR. EDWIN CRAFT

Am I(eye) the problem

In a broken world, can we learn to lay down our stones and love again

Copyright © 2025 by Dr. Edwin Craft

All rights reserved. No part of this publication may be reproduced, stored, or transmitted in any form or by any means, electronic, mechanical, photocopying, recording, scanning, or otherwise, without written permission from the publisher. It is illegal to copy this book, post it to a website, or distribute it by any other means without permission.

"*Scripture quotations are from the ESV® Bible (The Holy Bible, English Standard Version®), © 2001 by Crossway, a publishing ministry of Good News Publishers. ESV Text Edition: 2025. The ESV text may not be quoted in any publication made available to the public by a Creative Commons license. The ESV may not be translated in whole or in part into any other language. Used by permission. All rights reserved.*"

First edition

ISBN: 979-8-218-88955-5

To my wife Amy, you are my everything, my soulmate. I am so thankful that God placed us together for this journey in life. Each and every day is an adventure, and I love spending my life with you.

To my son Thomas, you are an amazing young man. Each day, I see how God is forming you and shaping you. I am so thankful that you are who you are. I am proud of you.

To my fellow pastors at FBC Cleveland, thank you for always being there and guiding me. It is great to have you around. You are my friends and my council.

To Brad, our lead pastor, our church shepherd, thank you for your teachings, your guidance, and your love for Christ. I am so grateful and honored to be able to learn and study under you.

Contents

Preface 1
Chapter 1: Introduction - The Vision of Christ 6
Chapter 2: The Red Lens of Love and Sacrifice 14
Chapter 3: The Blue Lens of Brokenness and Compassion 27
Chapter 4: The Gold Lens of Divine Worth 41
Chapter 5: The Green Lens of Growth and Transformation 56
Chapter 6: The Black Lens of Reality and Sin 69
Chapter 7: The White Lens of Purity and Restoration 86
Chapter 8: The Purple Lens of Royal Identity and Calling 99
Chapter 9: The Yellow Lens of Joy and Hope 112
Chapter 10: The Gray Lens of the In-Between 129
Chapter 11: The Multicolor Lens - The Full Spectrum of Grace 168
Chapter 12: Conclusion - Seeing Through His Eyes 183

Preface

It was bright one morning as I was driving, you know, one of those days when the sun pierces your windshield and for a moment blinds you. It was during one of those times that I had a brief panic attack because I couldn't see the road in front of me; it just disappeared. Even though I squinted to try to see, my path was momentarily blocked. Maybe you have experienced that as well, where your vision was impaired and you didn't know what to do next.

It was during one of those times that I frantically searched to find my sunglasses and put them on, and instantly, the tinted glasses caused the colors to shift and my vision to change. What had previously been a blinding light coming through my windshield quickly changed to a beautiful sunrise that only God can paint across the morning sky.

The view in front of me never changed; it was just the perspective I had that changed. The world remained exactly as God had intended it; my eyes just adjusted to see it a little differently, more in focus, and less blurred. I suddenly realized that many things in life can have huge impacts on our perspectives. That moment and many others like it began to weigh heavily on my heart and soul, and I began to think about how Jesus viewed the world. How did he view the woman at the well that we read about in John 4? I know that if I had been at the well the day that the young woman walked up, my perception of her would have probably been blurred by so many things. It would have been blurred by the baggage that had been established by years of my life experiences. I would have probably been influenced by things like tradition, rumors, other prior misconceptions, the clothing that she was wearing, her age, and maybe even her hygiene. As I began to think about that topic, I began to see something. What Jesus saw was not at all what I saw. He saw a lost soul that had been so ridiculed by life that she had to visit the well during the middle of the day, when no one else was around. She was haunted by life, by the perspective of others, people like me who couldn't see because they were blinded. Yes, as anyone would notice, she did walk in sin, but that wasn't the point. In this instance, even she wasn't the point; our perspective is. We all talk about others seeing Christ through us, but until we change the perspective of how we see others, then how will others be able to see Christ through our actions? If I had been at the well, what example would I have set for her to want to follow Christ? Would my gaze have been one that was helpful or hurtful? Would I have looked upon her as though I didn't carry my own baggage of sin on my shoulders? Would I have been carrying a "judgmental" stone, like the Pharisees in John 8, ready to hurl it at the slightest notion? Stones do two things. One, they make us the aggressors. Two, they weigh us down, both spiritually and physically.

You see, we are all wearing a set of glasses, filters, or lenses, if you may, just like the sunglasses that I put on to shield my eyes from the sun on that bright morning. To understand that more clearly, if you hold a red lens up and look through it, your perspective is changed, your view is tinted. But in life, our lenses are composed of experiences, biases, judgements, and misconceptions. Naturally, we filter the people around us and the world through those lenses. Sometimes we view them in black and white (judgment and suspicion). Other times, we filter them through rose-colored glasses, ignoring their struggles or sins. Sometimes we have blinders on, completely blocking them out as we walk right by. The fact is that thankfully, none of these perspectives comes close to how Jesus saw the world.

The question begs, how can we walk a sanctified life if we don't change the lens through which we look at the world? The Bible says in 1 Samuel 16:7, "The Lord does not view things the way we do. People look at the outward appearance, but the Lord looks at the heart." This is a powerful invitation to learn to see people the way Jesus sees them, through a spectrum of colors that illuminates their worth, their struggles, their potential, and their future.

This book is an invitation to change our perspective, to see the world a little differently. It is a journey into a spectrum full of colorful lenses that show both how we see the world today and a pathway to see the world more like Jesus. We will move through the rich colors of the gospel, the red of sacrifice, the blue of compassion, the gold of worth, the green of renewal, and discover how each color reveals a facet of His heart.

Instead of simplifying people into black-and-white judgments, we will learn to appreciate the way in which the Lord looks upon us. His view is not simplistic or shallow; it's rich, deep, purposeful, and loving.

The lenses that we discuss are two-way lenses; they see both the way that we look at others and the way that we look at ourselves. My hope and prayer is that, by the end of this book, you will begin to see yourself and those around you through His eyes, not ignoring sin or suffering but honoring the image of God in each person and extending the love of Christ to all.

> My hope and prayer is that, by the end of this book, you will begin to see yourself and those around you through His eyes, not ignoring sin or suffering but honoring the image of God in each person and extending the love of Christ to all.

One thing about reading this book, and I hope you take it to heart, l*iving out* a change in how we view the world is not a one-time decision; it's not read this book and now I am completely different. It is a process. It is going to be hard work. You wouldn't expect to go to the gym and immediately begin lifting the heaviest weight you can find. You would start small, build strength each day, and gradually increase what you can handle. The same is true with this book and applying the concepts in this book to your life. It is going to be a heavy lift. It may sometimes be a daily grind. But like a faithful athlete, you are going to have to hit the gym of life, and you are going to have to exercise your new eyes daily. Over time, what feels heavy today will grow lighter as your spirit is strengthened.

When you look back, you will understand that this was not just an exercise, but a plan for discipleship that begins to shape you into someone who begins to see through His eyes.

Chapter 1: Introduction - The Vision of Christ

> *1 Samuel 16:7 - But the Lord said to Samuel, "Do not look on his appearance or on the height of his stature, because I have rejected him. For the Lord sees not as man sees: man looks on the outward appearance, but the Lord looks on the heart."*

Imagine yourself for a moment walking on a crowded city street, and the hustle and bustle of life is in full swing. As you walk, people are all around you. The sights and sounds are immense. Maybe it's strangers walking beside you, or perhaps you have some of your closest friends brushing up against your sleeve. People pass briskly by, focused on life. A mom attempting to get a stain off a paint leg of a squirming kid. A dad is late for a meeting, hustling with a hot cup of coffee, each step, a few drops spill over the rim. An argument here, a kind word there. Each person wears a different style of clothing. Each one focused on a different path that would lead them somewhere else.

Listen as the noises fill the space around you. Maybe the blasting of a horn, the crying of a baby, a shout here, some type of construction going on in the background, as a hammer falls.

Are there any smells, maybe a freshly poured cup of coffee, or the smell of baking bread lingering in the street from the bakery just around the corner?

Now freeze your own picture in your mind. What do you see?

Let it really sink in as you think about the commotion that is going on around you. The shocking thing is that you probably never once thought about looking at your surroundings through the eyes of Jesus. You were probably way too consumed with everything else that your perspective wasn't quite clear. Often, that is the exact same way we wake up, we go through the day, and unfortunately, the way we return when we fall into bed exhausted. Consumed by life but not consumed by Christ.

> **Consumed by life but not consumed by Christ.**

Did you think about purpose? Why were you there at that moment in time? What did God have in store for you?

Now ask yourself one question: what would Jesus see? Don't scan quickly over this point, seriously, think about what Jesus would have seen. Even the disciples missed this point with the woman at the well.

John 4:27

27 Just then his disciples came back. They marveled that he was talking with a woman, but no one said, "What do you seek?" or, "Why are you talking with her?"

The disciples, upon returning and finding Jesus talking to the Samaritan woman, marveled, but stopped short of asking the question of why. They marveled at the thought of Jesus, the perfect savior, pausing for a moment to talk to an obvious sinner. Why would Jesus stop and talk to her? And why did no one ask the question? They had been walking with Jesus for a while, and they would have been comfortable asking the question, "Why are you talking with her?" They had asked many other questions. Maybe it was fear, or maybe they were just that oblivious to the fact that Jesus saw things differently. But Jesus was completely aware and went on to teach the disciples in verse 35:

35 Do you not say, 'There are yet four months, then comes the harvest'? Look, I tell you, lift up your eyes, and see that the fields are white for harvest.

Maybe we all need to just lift up our eyes

Lift up your eyes, gives the perception that the disciples were walking heads down, looking at their feet, unaware of things going on around them. Lift up your eyes, and see that the harvest is ready, because someone has already planted the seed. Lift up your eyes, and gaze upon what God has set before you. Lift up your eyes, and know that there is a plan in place. Lift up your eyes, and see that there is a purpose. Maybe we all need to just lift up our eyes and see.

Matthew 6:22-23 says:

22 The eye is the lamp of the body. So, if your eye is healthy, your whole body will be full of light, 23 but if your eye is bad, your whole body will be full of darkness. If then the light in you is darkness, how great is the darkness.

Many people interpret this to mean that the eyes are the gateway to the soul, which is only a partial truth of the scripture. The more complete truth lies in a deeper meaning concerning the spiritual and physical health of a person. The eye is a gateway, or as Matthew put it, a lamp to the whole body. And if it is a lamp to the whole body, then the body is illuminated by how the eyes are operating, in general terms what they see. Therefore, the eyes either create a body that is full of light or full of darkness. Let that sink in for a minute. What do the eyes do? They see. They give a perception of the world to the body, and the whole body is affected by what the eyes see.

Now, the interesting thing is that he moves from a healthy eye to an unhealthy eye. If he was talking about a physical issue such as blindness, then he would not be talking about the body being dark because of the blindness, so he must be focused on a spiritual state of the eye. A wrong perception of people or of the world can lead to a body that is full of darkness. A spiritual blindness can exist that leads to spiritual darkness. How did the disciples miss that they needed to lift up their eyes and see? How do we miss this?

Imagine for a moment if you had the opportunity to view that same scene above through the eyes of Jesus. Would your perception change? What would you see? Would looking through His eyes immediately tear through all the walls (lenses) that you have built up for years? Would the scales begin to fall from your eyes so that a spiritual awakening would begin to occur in your body?

How would others see you? Would they be able to turn the pages of your life, one by one, through the tears, the heartache, the pain? Would they be able to see the many times you have laughed, the other times that you have cried? What would they see? Would they see you differently?

The answer is yes, they would see differently, and you would see differently as well. And that is the point of this whole book. We don't need to passively sit by hoping that our perspective will change; we need to be able to rip the lenses from our eyes, much like the scales that fell off the eyes of Paul, when both his physical and spiritual blindness were lifted. In order for Paul to see spiritually, he had to be blinded physically, and when the physical blindness was lifted, then he began to see spiritually. In order for us to see spiritually, we need to understand how Jesus views humanity with humility.

For the purpose of getting a glimpse at how Jesus would have viewed the world, we are going to introduce colored lenses. Each lens or color represents a perspective that Jesus has in viewing us. A rather simplistic approach to viewing a complicated topic. We will explore the:

- Red lens of love and sacrifice
- Blue lens of brokenness and compassion
- Gold lens of divine worth

- Green lens of growth and transformation
- Black lens of reality and sin
- White lens of purity and restoration
- Purple lens of royal identity and calling
- Yellow lens of joy and hope
- Gray lens of in-between
- The multicolor lens of the full spectrum of grace

My hope is that as we walk through this together, we see the importance of seeing, not through our eyes but through His. As with the scripture above in Samuel, the Lord sees differently than man. I am so thankful that he does, and hopefully, when you finish this book, you will as well.

Reflection questions:

1. Have you ever thought about life in terms of how Jesus would have seen it?
2. Have you been seeing life through the right perspective?
3. As you look forward to future chapters, which lens are you most interested in?

Prayer:

Father,

As we read this book together, my hope would be that you reveal to us the baggage that we carry in seeing the world. That you would allow your Holy Spirit to guide us to see the world and ourselves differently. I pray that you will open our eyes to allow your spirit to shine its light on and through us.

Christ, your son, taught us the importance of seeing others differently. I pray that you will open our eyes to see as He saw the world, broken but worthy because of His sacrifice. Please fill our hearts with love and grace to see from a different perspective, to see the world through His eyes.

I pray that you will guide our steps and our paths as we begin to live out a new life. A life that you have given us. I pray for a renewed spirit, one that places you above all else. Grant us the ability and strength to serve you graciously.

Amen

Living it out:

- Your challenge for this week is to take one event, one moment in time, and pause for a minute to remember this chapter. Take a deep breath and answer the following:
    - What would Jesus see?
    - Why are you there?
    - What should you do?

Write about that experience here:

_____

_____

_____

_____

_____

_____

_____

_____

_____

_____

_____

Chapter 2: The Red Lens of Love and Sacrifice

John 15:13 Greater love has no one than this, that someone lay down his life for his friends.

Romans 5:8 but God shows his love for us in that while we were still sinners, Christ died for us.

God sees believers through the sacrifice of Christ's blood and unconditional love. Think of it as a lens that covers us so that when God looks at us, our sins are invisible, not because we did something that caused them to be removed, but because the covering of His blood allows God to see His children fully redeemed. The red lens completely changes the meaning of sacrifice. Ever notice how for the world to sacrifice anything is considered a loss, but to Jesus, it was for our gain? The world says protect yourself first; the bible says put your neighbor before yourself.

When Jesus looked at the world, He saw it through the **red lens of love and sacrifice**. Red is the color of blood, life given for another. To Jesus, love was not sentiment alone; it was costly, active, and always directed outward.

Seeing Through the Red Lens

Picture Jesus on the cross, tortured and bloody. He had been beaten, spit on, ridiculed, and mocked. He was a King, and there was never a doubt that He knew who He was. His eyes would have had to gaze across the crowd at the very ones who said crucify him. His perception would have allowed him to view past, present, and future sins of all that were there, and those of us yet to come. From the cross, Jesus should have seen the very worst of the world. From the cross, Jesus saw the crowd choose a thief and a murderer over Him. From that cross, He would have seen mine and your many shortcomings, but that was not what Jesus saw when He declared, *"Father, forgive them, for they know not what they do"* (Luke 23:34). Love, to Jesus, was not simply feeling compassion. It was not following what the world wanted Him to do. It was choosing sacrifice in the face of rejection.

Think for a moment how many times you may have walked away at the slightest resistance. Maybe it was in a relationship, a marriage, the most sacred of all covenants, when you chose yourself in front of your spouse. Maybe it was a friendship where you didn't or couldn't turn the other cheek. Your feelings were important, and they just didn't understand. There is no way that you would have admitted any wrongdoing at the time. We have all experienced times in life where we looked through the red lens of love and sacrifice as though it were the red lens of hate and narcissism.

> We have all experienced times in life where we looked through the red lens of love and sacrifice as though it were the red lens of hate and narcissism.

It is interesting that Jesus compares His relationship with the church to a marriage, and his friendship as worthy of laying down a life. But never once when faced with rejection did He hint at walking away. What we see are words like "Father, forgive them".

Proverbs 17:17 A friend loves at all times, and a brother is born for adversity.

John 15:13 "Greater love has no one than this, that someone lay down his life for his friends."

> Jesus taught us that love and sacrifice are inseparable.

Jesus teaches us that looking through the red lens is looking at the world differently. He taught us to look at a stranger with compassion instead of contempt. He taught us to look at a mother as loved, not lost. He taught us to look at a tax collector as worthy, not worthless. Jesus taught us that love and sacrifice are inseparable.

A Widow's Offering

Mark 12:41-44: And he sat down opposite the treasury and watched the people putting money into the offering box. Many rich people put in large sums. 42 And a poor widow came and put in two small copper coins, which make a penny. 43 And he called his disciples to him and said to them, "Truly, I say to you, this poor widow has put in more than all those who are contributing to the offering box. 44 For they all contributed out of their abundance, but she out of her poverty has put in everything she had, all she had to live on."

Jesus watched as people were giving their offerings at the temple. Don't miss the first action here, Jesus watched. He saw the wealthy put in large sums, and people admired their generosity. But Jesus was watching through His red lens. Jesus' eyes fell on a poor widow who dropped in two small copper coins. Take a moment and visualize this scene. As people went before her dropping in large sums of money, she walked up to the front. I can imagine that she was not dressed as well as the others. She probably didn't smile or laugh. She probably had her head down, looking at her feet as she slowly walked to the front. I wonder what was going through her mind. I know, if it were me, I would have probably been thinking about how I looked, what I was wearing, and about not measuring up to the others around me. You can almost hear the clink of the coins as they fall into the plate. Eyes watching, heads turning. The lens of the world would have gazed on the woman. Was it worth it for such a little offering? What was God going to do with that? It was small in comparison to what others were giving. To most, her gift would have been insignificant, just like how people saw her. But not to Jesus, you see, the scale was different. He wasn't measuring the value of her gift by its weight in gold. It was through the red lens of love and sacrifice that he saw her gift. She gave deeply, but she also gave in love. It was all that she had, and she was willing to give it through pain and heartache. The two small copper coins were costly, they were sacrificial, but most of all, they were given in love. God does not need your wealth; all of the wealth already belongs to Him.

> **Two things are evident: the disciples got to see for a moment through the red lens of Jesus and the woman demonstrated that love and sacrifice are bonded together.**

Two things are evident: the disciples got to see for a moment through the red lens of Jesus and the woman demonstrated that love and sacrifice are bonded together.

A Samaritan's Sacrifice

Luke 10:25-37 And behold, a lawyer stood up to put him to the test, saying, "Teacher, what shall I do to inherit eternal life?" 26 He said to him, "What is written in the Law? How do you read it?" 27 And he answered, "You shall love the Lord your God with all your heart and with all your soul and with all your strength and with all your mind, and your neighbor as yourself." 28 And he said to him, "You have answered correctly; do this, and you will live."

29 But he, desiring to justify himself, said to Jesus, "And who is my neighbor?" 30 Jesus replied, "A man was going down from Jerusalem to Jericho, and he fell among robbers, who stripped him and beat him and departed, leaving him half dead. 31 Now by chance a priest was going down that road, and when he saw him he passed by on the other side. 32 So likewise a Levite, when he came to the place and saw him, passed by on the other side. 33 But a Samaritan, as he journeyed, came to where he was, and when he saw him, he had compassion. 34 He went to him and bound up his wounds, pouring on oil and wine. Then he set him on his own animal and brought him to an inn and took care of him. 35 And the next day he took out two denarii[c] and gave them to the innkeeper, saying, 'Take care of him, and whatever more you spend, I will repay you when I come back.' 36 Which of these three, do you think, proved to be a neighbor to the man who fell among the robbers?" 37 He said, "The one who showed him mercy." And Jesus said to him, "You go, and do likewise."

In the parable of the Good Samaritan, we get a picture of the religious leaders passing by a wounded man on the side of the road. The man was obviously in need, and they of all people should have known love and sacrifice; however, all they saw was inconvenience, risk, and interruption. But along comes the unlikely hero, the Samaritan, despised by the Jewish society. In this parable, he saw differently. He saw a person in need, not because of the color of his skin, or his prestige in society, not because he had money, or would ever provide anything in return. He saw through the red lens of love and sacrifice.

Through the red lens, he poured oil and wine on the man's wounds. Through the red lens, he placed him on his own animal, instead of making him walk alongside. Through the red lens, he took him to the inn and paid for his care. This was not convenient love; it was costly, interrupting, sacrificial love.

That is how Jesus sees the world. Not through self-preservation, but through self-giving. He could have chosen to stay and give the earth many miracles through self-preservation, but through following the will of the Father, he gave us everything through His sacrifice on the cross.

The Cross: The Clearest Red Lens

Every act of compassion in Jesus' ministry pointed toward one ultimate expression, the cross. There, love and sacrifice meet in a full display of the red lens.

Paul writes in Romans 5:8, "But God shows his love for us in that while we were still sinners, Christ died for us."

The red lens changes the meaning of sacrifice. Sacrifice is not giving something up; it is gaining everything important.

The world says protect yourself first; Jesus says give willingly.

At Calvary, Jesus demonstrated that sacrificial love is not weakness but the greatest display of strength.

> **At Calvary, Jesus demonstrated that sacrificial love is not weakness but the greatest display of strength.**

Modern Red-Lens Living

Think of a parent who works two jobs, not for luxury but to put food on the table for their children. Think of a missionary who leaves behind comfort and luxury to serve in a dangerous place, a place where he may lose his life. Think of the mom who gives up her life and dreams to raise a wonderful child who was not expected. Think of a friend who forgives betrayal instead of retaliating. These are glimpses of Jesus' red lens lived out in our world.

To follow Jesus is to put the red lens on daily; to choose love that costs us something.

Living Through the Red Lens

So how do we see through this lens in our everyday lives?

- **Forgive deeply** - even when you've been hurt. Forgiveness is powerful. It frees us from the burden, baggage, resentment, and anger. It means letting go of past hurts and choosing to move forward. This could be directed inwardly to forgiveness of oneself, or outwardly to forgiveness

of others. Deep forgiveness can heal wounds and restore relationships, even when it is difficult. It releases us from the weight of owning the problem to freeing us to move forward with life.
- **Give generously** - not just from your surplus but sometimes from your need.

  Love and sacrifice will always go hand in hand. If you are loving without sacrifice, then your relationship is self-centered. Love should never be from just our surplus; it involves sharing what we have through sacrifice. It can be as simple as offering our time, which is one of our most important treasures. It could be offering a kind word when we have had a terrible day. It is about asking what you can give, not demanding what you want to receive. It is more about changing ourselves than changing others.
- **Serve humbly** - even when it means being unseen or unappreciated.

  Humble service goes a step further to putting others first without the expectation of receiving anything in return. It means performing an act of kindness quietly and sincerely, even when no one is watching. It is understanding that the well-being of others is important.
- **Love relentlessly** - even those who cannot love you back.

  This involves showing compassion, understanding, and kindness, even in the face of indifference or hostility. This love is "agape" love; it is unconditional and steadfast. It is transformative for both the giver and the receiver.

To love as Christ loves is not a human achievement; it is a divine miracle. The natural human response to offense, rejection, or betrayal is self-protection. The world teaches us to love those who love us, to give only when we receive something in return, and to measure affection by worthiness or reciprocity. Yet Jesus turned that logic upside down. He loved His enemies. He forgave those who crucified Him. He washed the feet of the one who would betray Him. This is not normal love; it is *supernatural love.*

This kind of love can only flow from a transformed heart, one empowered by the Holy Spirit. Romans 5:5 declares, *"God's love has been poured into our hearts through the Holy Spirit who has been given to us."* The Spirit of Christ takes what is impossible for our flesh and makes it possible by infusing us with divine capacity. The red lens, therefore, is not merely about learning to act lovingly; it is about being filled with Love from the Spirit.

When we walk by the Spirit (Galatians 5:16), one of the fruits of that Spirit, *love,* begins to take shape in us (Galatians 5:22). The Spirit softens hardened hearts, heals bitterness, and rewires the way we see others. Instead of seeing through the lens of offense, we begin to see through the lens of redemption. Instead of asking, "How do they deserve to be treated?" we ask, "How does Jesus see them?"

It is the Spirit of Christ who enables us to:

- **Love sacrificially**
- **Forgive freely**
- **Serve humbly**
- **Endure patiently**

This supernatural love does not originate within us; it flows *through* us. Like branches connected to the Vine (John 15:5), we bear fruit only because His life pulses within our veins. The Spirit transforms love from an act of duty into a reflection of divine identity, Christ in us, the hope of glory (Colossians 1:27).

Reflection Questions:

1. Who in your life right now needs to experience your love through sacrifice?
2. What one thing might Jesus ask you to lay down for the sake of others?
3. How does seeing love through the red lens change the way you think about the cross?

Prayer:

Father,

We are humbled by your love and your grace. We come before you with open hearts, seeking to open our eyes to live always seeing through the red lens of your love and sacrifice. Teach us each day to forgive deeply, even when we have been hurt. To forgive, just as You have forgiven us.

Help us to give generously, not only from our surplus, but also from our sacrifice, reflecting the selfless love that You have shown us. Grant us the grace to serve humbly, even when that service goes unnoticed or unappreciated, knowing that we serve You and You see all things.

Fill our hearts with love toward others, even though some will never return the love to us. Let us live our lives as a testament to your sacrificial love and allow the world to see your love through our actions.

Strengthen us to persevere and to choose love and sacrifice over anger and hate. We ask all these things in the name of Jesus, who loved us even when we shouldn't have been, who showed grace when we did not deserve it, and who sacrificed His precious life so that we might live.

Amen.

Living it out:

Take a normal instance this week and turn it into something Christ-centered. It can't be just a normal area of service; it must be something sacrificial. Take something that is precious to you, probably money or time, and devote it to something sacrificial for someone else other than yourself.

- What was the result?
- How did this help further the Kingdom?

Use the space below to write about your experience:

_____

_____

_____

_____

_____

_____

_____

_____

_____

Chapter 3: The Blue Lens of Brokenness and Compassion

Matthew 9:36 When he saw the crowds, he had compassion for them, because they were harassed and helpless, like sheep without a shepherd.

Luke 7:13 And when the Lord saw her, he had compassion on her and said to her, "Do not weep."

The older I get, the more funerals I seem to be attending. Funerals are one of those places that give us a deep picture of hurting and grieving people. Grief over the loss of a loved one is a painful experience. It is at those times that I find myself the most lost, searching for words that don't exist. Trying to mumble something that will ease the pain. I'll pray for you. We are going to miss him/her. He/she was a great person. We will see them again someday in Heaven. Words that are hopeful but still, for some reason, remain empty when compared to the measuring scale of grief. True grief is never fleeting. It lingers for days, months, and years. To be honest, I struggle with how to handle grief when confronted by it.

But when Jesus looked at the world, He saw its brokenness, and His heart moved with compassion. The Bible does not contain a verse where it says He turned away from pain, but there are many where He willingly entered into it.

Seeing Through the Blue Lens

The Bible is full of imperfect situations that make it so perfect. It is truly God breathed, because if it were written by an uninspired person, it would be full of perfect stories about perfect people. But God's word gives us hope in the midst of pain, and we see hope through the lens of brokenness and compassion.

Lazarus

John 11 Now a certain man was ill, Lazarus of Bethany, the village of Mary and her sister Martha. 2 It was Mary who anointed the Lord with ointment and wiped his feet with her hair, whose brother Lazarus was ill. 3 So the sisters sent to him, saying, "Lord, he whom you love is ill." 4 But when Jesus heard it he said, "This illness does not lead to death.

It is for the glory of God, so that the Son of God may be glorified through it."

5 Now Jesus loved Martha and her sister and Lazarus. 6 So, when he heard that Lazarus was ill, he stayed two days longer in the place where he was. 7 Then after this he said to the disciples, "Let us go to Judea again." 8 The disciples said to him, "Rabbi, the Jews were just now seeking to stone you, and are you going there again?" 9 Jesus answered, "Are there not twelve hours in the day? If anyone walks in the day, he does not stumble, because he sees the light of this world. 10 But if anyone walks in the night, he stumbles, because the light is not in him." 11 After saying these things, he said to them, "Our friend Lazarus has fallen asleep, but I go to awaken him." 12 The disciples said to him, "Lord, if he has fallen asleep, he will recover." 13 Now Jesus had spoken of his death, but they thought that he meant taking rest in sleep. 14 Then Jesus told them plainly, "Lazarus has died, 15 and for your sake I am glad that I was not there, so that you may believe. But let us go to him." 16 So Thomas, called the Twin, said to his fellow disciples, "Let us also go, that we may die with him." 17 Now when Jesus came, he found that Lazarus had already been in the tomb four days. 18 Bethany was near Jerusalem, about two miles off, 19 and many of the Jews had come to Martha and Mary to console them concerning their brother. 20 So when Martha heard that Jesus was coming, she went and met him, but Mary remained seated in the house. 21 Martha said to Jesus, "Lord, if you had been here, my brother would not have died. 22 But even now I know that whatever you ask from God, God will give you." 23 Jesus said to her, "Your brother will rise again." 24 Martha said to him, "I know that he will rise again in the resurrection on the last day." 25 Jesus said to her, "I am the resurrection and the life. Whoever believes in me, though he die, yet shall he live, 26 and everyone who lives and believes in me shall never die. Do you believe this?" 27 She said to him, "Yes, Lord; I believe that you are the Christ, the Son of God, who is coming into the world."

When Jesus said, *"Lazarus has died, and for your sake I am glad I was not there, so that you may believe"* (John 11:14-15), it was an unexpected statement. His words revealed both divine purpose and deep compassion. Lazarus's death was not meaningless; it was a moment Jesus would use to strengthen the faith of those closest to Him.

Like the disciples, we often struggle to see that purpose in our own grief. Even when we pray for strength, that strength can feel just out of reach. The disciples were in that very place, confused, weary, and walking in what Jesus described as *darkness* (v.10). He feared they would stumble, not because they lacked love for Him, but because pain can easily cloud our vision.

Death has a way of dimming the light around us. It can invite a quiet darkness to creep into our hearts, blurring our hope and distorting our trust. Yet through the blue lens of compassion, we see that Jesus does not leave us there. Even in our sorrow, He walks with us, turning moments of loss into opportunities for deeper belief and renewed faith.

> We should find comfort shown by His compassion. We should find comfort in His words. Most of all, we should also find comfort in His presence. And this truth is important: He is always present for His children.

One could see where the disciples may have allowed that darkness to turn into sarcasm as they responded to Jesus not with "We will follow you to the ends of the earth", but *"Let us all go, that we may die with him."* Sarcasm or sincere devotion? If sarcasm, it is something we would expect from a teenager, not something we would expect from the future leaders of the church. However, Jesus saw death as not the ending, but the beginning, and He used this as a teaching moment for His close, but possibly sarcastic disciples. When He arrived, He spoke these beautiful words, *"I am the resurrection and the life. Whoever believes in me, though he die, yet shall he live."* We should find comfort shown by His compassion. We should find comfort in His words. Most of all, we should also find comfort in His presence. And this truth is important: He is always present for His children.

Jesus wept over Jerusalem

Yes, Jesus showed emotion. He cried. One of the shortest verses in the bible came just a few short verses behind where we left off in the story of Lazarus above. John 11:35, "Jesus wept." The memorization verse that we all learned as children. But He did, He cried for Humanity because he saw the broken world through the blue lens of compassion.

Luke 19:37-44 As he was drawing near—already on the way down the Mount of Olives—the whole multitude of his disciples began to rejoice and praise God with a loud voice for all the mighty works that they had seen, [38] saying, "Blessed is the King who comes in the name of the Lord! Peace in heaven and glory in the highest!" [39] And some of the Pharisees in the crowd said to him, "Teacher, rebuke your disciples." [40] He answered, "I tell you, if these were silent, the very stones would cry out."

[41] And when he drew near and saw the city, he wept over it, [42] saying, "Would that you, even you, had known on this day the things that make for peace! But now they are hidden from your eyes. [43] For the days will come upon you, when your enemies will set up a barricade around you and surround you and hem you in on every side [44] and tear you down to the ground, you and your children within you. And they will not leave one stone upon another in you, because you did not know the time of your visitation."

During the celebration, Jesus saw the world through the blue lens, and His statement here is so powerful. "If you, even you, had only known on this day what would bring you peace," and don't miss what comes next. "but now they are hidden from your eyes." Understand that the blue lens of compassion did not exist for the eyes of the Pharisees. They were blinded, scales over their eyes. It was right there in front of them; destruction was ahead. But they were blinded. If only they would just open their eyes to see that the glory of the Lord is right before them. If only we would open our eyes as well, we could see.

A Woman's Tears

Consider the sinful woman who wept at Jesus' feet

Luke 7:36-50 One of the Pharisees asked him to eat with him, and he went into the Pharisee's house and reclined at table. 37 And behold, a woman of the city, who was a sinner, when she learned that he was reclining at table in the Pharisee's house, brought an alabaster flask of ointment, 38 and standing behind him at his feet, weeping, she began to wet his feet with her tears and wiped them with the hair of her head and kissed his feet and anointed them with the ointment. 39 Now when the Pharisee who had invited him saw this, he said to himself, "If this man were a prophet, he would have known who and what sort of woman this is who is touching him, for she is a sinner." 40 And Jesus answering said to him, "Simon, I have something to say to you." And he answered, "Say it, Teacher."

41 "A certain moneylender had two debtors. One owed five hundred denarii, and the other fifty. 42 When they could not pay, he cancelled the debt of both. Now which of them will love him more?" 43 Simon answered, "The one, I suppose, for whom he cancelled the larger debt." And he said to him, "You have judged rightly." 44 Then turning toward the woman he said to Simon, "Do you see this woman? I entered your house; you gave me no water for my feet, but she has wet my feet with her tears and wiped them with her hair. 45 You gave me no kiss, but from the time I came in she has not ceased to kiss my feet. 46 You did not anoint my head with oil, but she has anointed my feet with ointment. 47 Therefore I tell you, her sins, which are many, are forgiven—for she loved much. But he who is forgiven little, loves little." 48 And he said to her, "Your sins are forgiven." 49 Then those who were at table with him began to say among[h] themselves, "Who is this, who even forgives sins?" 50 And he said to the woman, "Your faith has saved you; go in peace."

She was broken, ashamed, and rejected by her community. Her reputation preceded her; whispers followed wherever she went. To the world, she was a sinner beyond redemption, a name to be avoided, not embraced. Yet through the *blue lens* of compassion, Jesus did not see her as damaged goods. He looked beyond her past and saw the image of God still glimmering beneath the layers of guilt and rejection.

Where others saw scandal, Jesus saw sincerity. Her tears, falling freely at His feet, were not signs of disgrace but of worship. Every drop carried a story of repentance, a longing to be known and loved despite her failures. Her brokenness became the very soil in which forgiveness could take root. It was not her perfection that drew His attention, but her posture, her humility, became the open door through which redemption could enter.

Through the blue lens, we see what divine compassion truly looks like. Jesus didn't excuse her sin; He addressed it with truth wrapped in mercy. He saw her not for what she had done but for what she could become in Him. Where others turned away in judgment, He turned toward her in grace. Where they saw a woman ruined by sin, He saw a daughter ready to be restored.

> **Where others turned away in judgment, He turned toward her in grace. Where they saw a woman ruined by sin, He saw a daughter ready to be restored.**

This is the heart of Christ's compassion; it redefines worth through love. His gaze transforms shame into dignity, pain into purpose, and tears into testimonies. The blue lens reminds us that Jesus meets us not at the height of our strength, but in the depth of our need. Compassion does not ignore brokenness; it redeems it. While others saw sin, Jesus saw a daughter ready to be restored.

Brokenness Moved Him

Over and over, the Gospels tell us that when Jesus saw the crowds, *"He had compassion on them"* (Matthew 9:36). He saw people not as problems to solve, but as sheep without a shepherd, wandering, hurting, and vulnerable. He was present, always present.

- When the leper approached Him and said, *"If you will, you can make me clean"* (Mark 1:40), Jesus

was *"moved with pity"* and touched the man others would never dare to touch.
- When the hungry had no food, His compassion fed them.
- When the blind cried out, His compassion restored their sight.

Through the blue lens, brokenness was not an inconvenience to Jesus. It didn't mess up his day; it was an invitation. He openly welcomed it to display the heart of God, to allow His light to shine brightly.

The Compassion of the Cross

At the cross, Jesus displayed not only sacrificial love (the red lens) but also deep compassion (the blue lens). Hanging in agony, He looked upon His mother and made plans for her care (John 19:26-27). He heard the criminal beside Him and spoke words of assurance: *"Today you will be with me in paradise"* (Luke 23:43). Even in His own suffering, His eyes searched for those who needed comfort.

The blue lens reveals that compassion is not withheld by our own pain; it becomes more clear because of it.

Seeing through the lens

When we put on the blue lens, we begin to see people differently:

- The homeless man on the street is not a nuisance, but a person with an important life and a soul.
- The addict or alcoholic is not a statistic, but someone carrying wounds deeper than we can see.

- The grieving widow is not just another face in the pew, but a soul who needs our time more than our words.

Compassion requires slowing down, joining into another's brokenness, and offering presence even when solutions are not possible.

Through the blue lens, Jesus reminds us that brokenness is not the end, but compassion is the pathway to healing.

Living Through the Blue Lens

To follow Jesus is to cultivate eyes that see hurt and hearts that react with compassion.

- **Listen more than you speak** - compassion begins with presence.
  True compassion starts with being fully present for others. This means actively listening without interrupting or planning your response. When we listen more than we speak, it means we value what the other person has to say.
- **Join in others' pain** - don't run from tears, sit and cry with them.
  Even though it is hard, compassion involves sharing in others' pain. Instead of hiding from pain, we should be willing to sacrifice to sit with someone through their pain. This might mean crying with them, or hurting with them, but most of all it will mean spending time with them.
- **Be generous with mercy** - people need kindness more than correction.

In moments of struggle or pain, people need to be freely given mercy more than advice or correction. Being generous with mercy means being able to provide understanding and kindness, even when it may be easier to judge and criticize. This does not mean that if someone is living in sin, that we overlook it, but that we provide a merciful ear for them to feel safe talking to.

- **Pray with open hearts** - lifting the broken to the One who heals.

Prayer is a powerful way to show compassion, especially when we lift up those who are hurting. Praying with an open heart means being sincere and earnest in our prayers, asking God for healing, comfort, and strength. It acknowledges that we do not have the answers, but that we trust in the One that does.

Reflection Questions:

1. When was the last time someone's brokenness moved you to compassion?
2. How can you slow down enough to notice the hurting people around you?
3. What might change in your relationships if you looked at others through Jesus' blue lens?

Prayer:

Father,

Please help me to see through the blue lens of brokenness and compassion. Please allow this to be a new ministry in my life where I am able to give freely of my time, my compassion, and my presence to listen to others as they go through hardships and pain. To help them see You during times of their hardships and struggles. Please help me to embrace the pain as brothers(sisters) in Christ. Please allow the scales of this world to be removed from my eyes so that I see as You saw, that brokenness is not the ending, but a new beginning.

We know this world is flawed, but we also have the promise that You have gone to prepare a place that has no more sorrow and no more tears. Help us to show the compassion that You demonstrated to others as we walk through this life. It is in your Holy name that we pray. Amen.

Living it out:

Allow the blue lens of compassion to consume you this week. Seek out someone in need, someone who is hurting, and just sit with them. Words aren't as important as time. Allow them to do most of the talking, understanding that silence can be ok as well. Don't try to comfort them with a story about yourself; remember, you are not the most important person in the room.

- Did you find the overall experience painful or purposeful?
- What was the outcome? How do you feel about the experience?

Use the space below to write about your experience.

_____

_____

_____

_____

_____

_____

_____

_____

_____

_____

_____

_____

Chapter 4: The Gold Lens of Divine Worth

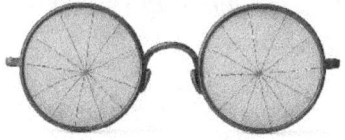

Luke 15

The Lost Coin

The Lost Sheep

The Lost Son

Gold has always given a false impression of a sense of self-worth, an elevation of value above others. Some people value their lives based on the amount of treasure they have built up here on earth. It is interesting that as currencies have changed, ruling parties have shifted, and gold has always been perceived as wealth. To every culture, authority, or civilization, it is precious, rare, and enduring.

In Revelation 3:17-18, we are taught:

"For you say, "I am rich, I have prospered, and I need nothing," not realizing that you are wretched, pitiable, poor, bland, and naked. I counsel you to buy from me gold refined by fire, so that you may be rich, and white garments so that you may clothe yourself and the shame of your nakedness may not be seen, and salve to anoint your eyes, so that you may see."

As Jesus spoke to the seven churches in Revelation, we get a picture of worth when we gaze at the church of Laodicea. The church of Laodicea had become lukewarm, placing its value in the wealth that it had created for itself. Sometimes it is in these moments when we value ourselves more than we should or attempt to place ourselves higher than we should that we can be the most blinded. Jesus points them to the fact that even though they believe that they are rich, they are poor and naked. He directs them to purchase salve so that they can see. Salve that will remove the lens so that they can see the true picture that Jesus saw. When Jesus looked at people, He saw them through the gold lens of divine worth, not the gold lens of self-worth. He did not measure them by status, wealth, success, or failure. Instead, He looked deeply, beyond the superficial, to the eternal value placed upon them by God himself. The value that God sees in a soul, your soul, is worth more than all the gold on earth.

The Image of God

In Genesis 1:27, we are told:

"So God created man in his own image, in the image of God he created him; male and female he created them."

From the beginning, humanity was crowned with glory, created in the image of God. Sin blurred that image but did not erase it. It was only because of Jesus through His death, burial, and resurrection, His blood spilt for ours, that our image is clear to God, without blemish. Jesus came not only to redeem us from sin, but to restore us as His children with a redeemed standing to be in His presence.

When He looked at people, He did not see what society saw. He saw the divine imprint that was meant from the beginning of time. He saw the image of God in each of us.

> He saw the divine imprint that was meant from the beginning of time. He saw the image of God in each of us.

Seeing Value Where Others Saw None

- **The children** - When the disciples tried to push children aside as unimportant, Jesus rebuked them and said, *"Let the little children come to me… for to such belongs the kingdom of heaven"* (Matthew 19:14). In a culture that dismissed children, Jesus saw gold.

- **The outcast** - When society avoided lepers, tax collectors, and sinners, Jesus sought them out. He ate with Zacchaeus, touched the leper, and defended the woman caught in adultery. When others saw shame, Jesus saw worth.

- **The poor widow** - We met her through the red lens of sacrifice, but here we see her through the gold lens as well: overlooked by men, but honored by the Lord as one who gave more than all the rich combined.

In Luke, we get a picture of lost items and their worth, the lost coin, the lost sheep, and then the lost son.

The Lost Sheep

Perhaps the clearest picture of the gold lens is in Jesus' parable of the lost sheep (Luke 15:3-7).

So he told them this parable: 4 "What man of you, having a hundred sheep, if he has lost one of them, does not leave the ninety-nine in the open country, and go after the one that is lost, until he finds it? 5 And when he has found it, he lays it on his shoulders, rejoicing. 6 And when he comes home, he calls together his friends and his neighbors, saying to them, 'Rejoice with me, for I have found my sheep that was lost.' 7 Just so, I tell you, there will be more joy in heaven over one sinner who repents than over ninety-nine righteous persons who need no repentance.

Ninety-nine were safe, but one wandered. To most, losing one out of a hundred seems like an acceptable risk. After all, what is one sheep worth when you have ninety-nine more to tend? Is it really worth the trouble, the energy, the risk of leaving the others behind? Logic would say no, but His love says otherwise.

Through the *gold lens*, Jesus reveals something far deeper: that every soul carries immeasurable worth in the eyes of God.

> **To the Shepherd, each sheep is personal, known by name, and loved beyond measure.**

While the world will place value based on numbers, productivity, and performance, He places value in an intimate relationship. To the Shepherd, each sheep is personal, known by name, and loved beyond measure. The loss of even one creates a gap that cannot be filled by the ninety-nine who remain.

When Jesus tells this parable in Luke 15, He is addressing those who grumbled that He welcomed sinners and ate with them. But what they missed was the *gold,* the pure, radiant love that drives Heaven to pursue the one who strays. In human eyes, that pursuit looks inefficient. In divine eyes, it is essential. Every person, no matter how far they have wandered, reflects the golden imprint of God's image and is worth the journey of redemption.

When the Shepherd finds the lost sheep, He does not scold it or drive it back to the fold. He lifts it onto His shoulders with joy and carries it home. That moment captures the heart of the Gospel, our value is not determined by what we bring to God, but by what He has invested in us through His love. Jesus concludes, *"Rejoice with me, for I have found my sheep that was lost."* (Luke 15:6)

Through the gold lens, we are reminded that in God's kingdom, no one is disposable. Every soul matters. Every wanderer is worth the search. The gold lens glows with the radiance of divine worth; it reveals a God who does not weigh our value by our usefulness, but by His unchanging affection.

Heaven's joy is not found in safety or statistics, but in restoration. The ninety-nine are loved. but the one who returns shines with the brilliance of redemption.

The Lost Coin
Luke 15:8-10

8 "Or what woman, having ten silver coins, if she loses one coin, does not light a lamp and sweep the house and seek diligently until she finds it? 9 And when she has found it, she calls together her friends and neighbors, saying, 'Rejoice with me, for I have found the coin that I had lost.' 10 Just so, I tell you, there is joy before the angels of God over one sinner who repents."

Next, Jesus tells the story of a woman who loses one of her ten silver coins. To most, the loss might seem small, a single coin among many. But to her, it was precious. She lights a lamp, sweeps the floor, and searches *diligently* until she finds it.

The coin had value that was given to it. A 100-dollar bill has value to us, not because of the actual paper that it is made with; any bill could be made from that paper. The face that is on the front of that bill gives it value. We have also been stamped or sealed, in the beginning we were created in the image of God (*Imago Dei*) and then as His children, we have been sealed with the Holy Spirit.

Ephesians 1:13-14 shows us that:

13 In him you also, when you heard the word of truth, the gospel of your salvation, and believed in him, were sealed with the promised Holy Spirit, 14 who is the guarantee of our inheritance until we acquire possession of it, to the praise of his glory.

The striking addition in this parable, compared to the lost sheep, is the widening circle of joy. Not only does the woman call together her friends and neighbors to celebrate, but Jesus reveals that Heaven itself joins the rejoicing. *"There is joy before the angels of God over one sinner who repents."* (v.10)

Through the *gold lens of worth*, this scene shimmers with meaning. It is as though Heaven bends low to watch redemption unfold on earth. Each time a lost soul is found, the light of God's glory reflects through the golden lens, illuminating the infinite value He places on every person. The angels, who have seen the vastness of creation and the majesty of God's throne, still rejoice over one repentant heart, because that heart bears the image of the Creator Himself.

The woman's careful search mirrors the heart of God. She refuses to rest until the lost is found. She lights the lamp, a symbol of divine illumination, representing God's relentless pursuit through the light of His Spirit. Her sweeping of the house shows God's attention to every hidden place, every dark corner of a life that feels forgotten. Nothing is too small or insignificant for His care.

> **Every life, no matter how buried or overlooked, gleams with divine worth. And when the light of grace touches that life, Heaven erupts in joy, for what was lost has been found.**

What a beautiful image this gives us of how Heaven looks upon humanity through the golden lens: not with judgment or distance, but with delight. Every life, no matter how buried or overlooked, gleams with divine worth. And when the light of grace touches that life, Heaven erupts in joy, for what was lost has been found.

The Lost Son
Luke 15:11-32

11 And he said, "There was a man who had two sons. 12 And the younger of them said to his father, 'Father, give me the share of property that is coming to me.' And he divided his property between them. 13 Not many days later, the younger son gathered all he had and took a journey into a far country, and there he squandered his property in reckless living. 14 And when he had spent everything, a severe famine arose in that country, and he began to be in need. 15 So he went and hired himself out to one of the citizens of that country, who sent him into his fields to feed pigs. 16 And he was longing to be fed with the pods that the pigs ate, and no one gave him anything.

17 "But when he came to himself, he said, 'How many of my father's hired servants have more than enough bread, but I perish here with hunger! 18 I will arise and go to my father, and I will say to him, "Father, I have sinned against heaven and before you. 19 I am no longer worthy to be called your son. Treat me as one of your hired servants."' 20 And he arose and came to his father. But while he was still a long way off, his father saw him and felt compassion, and ran and embraced him and kissed him. 21 And the son said to him, 'Father, I have sinned against heaven and before you. I am no longer worthy to be called your son.' 22 But the father said to his servants, 'Bring quickly the best robe, and put it on him, and put a ring on his hand, and shoes on his feet. 23 And bring the fattened calf and kill it, and let us eat and celebrate. 24 For this my son was dead, and is alive again; he was lost, and is found.' And they began to celebrate.

25 "Now his older son was in the field, and as he came and drew near to the house, he heard music and dancing. 26 And he called one of the servants and asked what these things meant. 27 And he said to him, 'Your brother has come, and your father has killed the fattened calf, because he has received him back safe and sound.' 28 But he was angry and refused to go in. His father came out and entreated him, 29 but he answered his father, 'Look, these many years I have served you, and I never disobeyed your command, yet you never gave me a

> *young goat, that I might celebrate with my friends. 30 But when this son of yours came, who has devoured your property with prostitutes, you killed the fattened calf for him!' 31 And he said to him, 'Son, you are always with me, and all that is mine is yours. 32 It was fitting to celebrate and be glad, for this your brother was dead, and is alive; he was lost, and is found.'"*

Of the three parables in Luke 15, the story of the lost son is the most personal and profound. It reaches deeper than the lost sheep or the lost coin, because here the "lost" one is not an animal or an object; it is a person who chooses to walk away. The gold lens helps us not only to see the world with God's eyes, but also to see ourselves through His heart of compassion and value.

One of the hardest truths for us to accept is that we, too, are worth pursuing. We often find it easy to affirm that others have value, but difficult to believe the same about ourselves, especially when we are standing in the wreckage of our own choices. When we've fallen into sin, disappointment, or shame, the reflection we see in the mirror often feels unworthy of love. Yet through the gold lens, God sees past the stains of our past to the potential of our redemption.

The prodigal son reached a moment of utter humiliation, alone, hungry, and feeding pigs in a foreign land. It was there, at his lowest point, that he began to remember the goodness of his father. That memory stirred something holy within him: a faint glimmer of worth that sin had tried to bury. His decision to

> **Through this lens, we learn that our worth is not found in what we've done, but in *whose* we are.**

return home was not born out of arrogance, but from the faint hope that maybe, just maybe, his father would still see him as worth receiving.

The beauty of the gold lens is that it reveals both sides of this story: the father and the sons. The father, representing God, runs to meet the returning son, not with condemnation, but with compassion. He clothes him in a robe, places a ring on his hand, and restores his place in the family. Every action radiates value. The son thought he was returning to beg for mercy; instead, he was welcomed into the full warmth of love. Through this lens, we learn that our worth is not found in what we've done, but in *whose* we are.

But the gold lens also compels us to look at the older son, the one who stayed home, followed the rules, and yet grew resentful when grace was given to someone he deemed undeserving. His self-righteousness blinded him to the same mercy that covered his brother. The gold lens reveals that both sons were lost in different ways: one through rebellion, the other through pride. Both needed to rediscover their worth in the Father's grace.

True worth, then, is not something we earn or display; it is something we *receive*. It humbles us rather than inflates us.

To see ourselves through the gold lens is to remember both where we came from and what we've been redeemed for. It means holding the memory of the filth we once wallowed in without letting it define us, because grace has rewritten our story.

The gold lens teaches us to rejoice in restoration, not in comparison. It reminds us that the Father's love is not divided among His children; it is multiplied. The same grace that restores the wayward son also invites the faithful son to share in the joy of reconciliation. Through this lens, we learn that every soul, rebellious or religious, has immeasurable worth, not because of what we bring to God, but because of what Christ has already done for us.

The Cross: Gold Revealed Through Blood

It is at the cross that we get a clear picture of seeing through the gold lens. Peter reminds us in 1 Peter 1:18-19:

"You were ransomed… not with perishable things such as silver or gold, but with the precious blood of Christ."

The cross is the ultimate statement of our worth. Jesus would not have shed His blood for worthless things. He laid down His life because He saw divine worth in us. Divine worth is measured not by our works, but by the ransom price, the price that He paid through His blood, for our souls.

Living Through the Gold Lens

When we put on the gold lens, we begin to see people the way Jesus did:

- The coworker who is annoying, but was created in the image of God.
- The stranger on the street that Christ deemed worth dying for.
- The marginalized, the overlooked, the forgotten are all treasures in God's sight.

To see through the gold lens is to treat people not according to what they deserve, but according to the worth God has already given them. The grace that has been freely given to us by the King is also available to them.

Reflection Questions

1. How does the truth that you were "bought with a price" reshape the way you see your own worth?
2. Who in your life have you undervalued that God might be calling you to see through His gold lens?
3. How can your words and actions affirm the divine worth in others this week?

Prayer:

Father,

We ask that You help us see the world through the gold lens. To recognize the divine worth of both ourselves and others, and that you did not create anything ordinary. Let us appreciate the blessings that you have given us each day. May this lens not just be a symbol of Your glory, but a reminder of the precious gift of life that You have given us.

Grant us the wisdom to see beyond the surface in people and to understand the deeper truths. Let us embrace the journey of growth and transformation. Help us to encourage and uplift others around us, to be patient and kind, and to invest in the discipleship of those around us.

Let us each and every day celebrate the sanctification process, knowing that every step we take is a testament to Christ. May we always give thanks for Your transforming power.

Amen

Living it out:

Question 2 above asks that you identify a person in your life that you may have undervalued. Maybe it is a spouse, a father or a mother, or maybe it is your neighbor. Whoever you identified, use this week to do something special for that person that demonstrates their worth.

Write down how they accepted your actions.

_____

_____

_____

_____

_____

_____

_____

_____

_____

_____

_____

Chapter 5: The Green Lens of Growth and Transformation

John 15:1-8 "I am the true vine, and my Father is the vinedresser. ² Every branch in me that does not bear fruit he takes away, and every branch that does bear fruit he prunes, that it may bear more fruit. ³ Already you are clean because of the word that I have spoken to you. ⁴ Abide in me, and I in you. As the branch cannot bear fruit by itself, unless it abides in the vine, neither can you, unless you abide in me. ⁵ I am the vine; you are the branches. Whoever abides in me and I in him, he it is that bears much fruit, for apart from me you can do nothing. ⁶ If anyone does not abide in me, he is thrown away like a branch and withers; and the branches are gathered, thrown into the fire, and

> burned. *⁷ If you abide in me, and my words abide in you, ask whatever you wish, and it will be done for you. ⁸ By this my Father is glorified, that you bear much fruit and so prove to be my disciples.*
>
> *2 Corinthians 5:17 Therefore, if anyone is in Christ, he is a new creation.[c] The old has passed away; behold, the new has come.*

I always love springtime, especially after coming out of a cold, wet, and gloomy winter. The first sprouts of green grass reveal that new life is on the way. Soon, birds will be singing, flowers will be blooming, and we will get a little peek at the greatness of God. Green is a sign of fresh beginnings and new things to come. I often imagine a seed struggling to push through the dirt in the springtime, the slight bend to its trunk as it begins to emerge, fragile and weak, but at the same time full of life. That little shoot of a plant may grow into a wonderful flower, or a healthy tomato, or even a towering tree. Only its creator knows what it will become. Over time, that little tree will receive nutrients from the soil, sun from the sky, and water from the air. It will grow and become stronger to fulfill its purpose.

When Jesus looks at people, I believe that he sees the same thing: what he created us to be, not necessarily as we are now, but what we are to become. Through the green lens of growth and transformation, He sees potential, progress, and a future that can only be reshaped by the power of God.

The Seed and the Soil

Jesus often spoke about growth through parables of seeds and harvests. One of His most famous is the parable of the sower:

Matthew 13:3-17 That same day Jesus went out of the house and sat beside the sea. 2 And great crowds gathered about him, so that he got into a boat and sat down. And the whole crowd stood on the beach. 3 And he told them many things in parables, saying: "A sower went out to sow. 4 And as he sowed, some seeds fell along the path, and the birds came and devoured them. 5 Other seeds fell on rocky ground, where they did not have much soil, and immediately they sprang up, since they had no depth of soil, 6 but when the sun rose they were scorched. And since they had no root, they withered away. 7 Other seeds fell among thorns, and the thorns grew up and choked them. 8 Other seeds fell on good soil and produced grain, some a hundredfold, some sixty, some thirty. 9 He who has ears, let him hear."

10 Then the disciples came and said to him, "Why do you speak to them in parables?" 11 And he answered them, "To you it has been given to know the secrets of the kingdom of heaven, but to them it has not been given. 12 For to the one who has, more will be given, and he will have an abundance, but from the one who has not, even what he has will be taken away. 13 This is why I speak to them in parables, because seeing they do not see, and hearing they do not hear, nor do they understand. [14] *Indeed, in their case the prophecy of Isaiah is fulfilled that says:*

"You will indeed hear but never understand,
and you will indeed see but never perceive."
[15] *For this people's heart has grown dull,*
and with their ears they can barely hear,
and their eyes they have closed,
lest they should see with their eyes
and hear with their ears
and understand with their heart
and turn, and I would heal them.

[16] *But blessed are your eyes, for they see, and your ears, for they hear.* [17] *For truly, I say to you, many prophets and righteous people longed to see what you see, and did not see it, and to hear what you hear, and did not hear it.*

Take a moment and count the number of times that Jesus used the terms "eyes" and "see" in the preceding verses.

Notice verse 13, *"seeing they do not see."* How many days do we walk through life seeing but not seeing? Their eyes, they have grown dull…and their eyes have closed, giving the perception that at one time, their eyes were open, with the ability to see. However, over time, they became dull, clouded.

I heard Jerry Clower once spin a yarn about a frog in a skillet. Based on research, it was traditionally more of a fable, but hearing him tell it really drove home the point of how we can become clouded and dulled over time. The story went something like this:

> Once upon a time, a man wished to see how a frog would react to danger.
> He took a live frog and dropped it into a pot of boiling water.
> The instant the frog touched the water, it gave a mighty leap and sprang out.
> It knew at once that it was in danger, and it escaped with its life.
>
> Then the man took another frog and placed it in a pot of cool, still water.
> The frog was comfortable there and did not try to leave.
> The man set the pot upon the fire and let the water warm slowly.
>
> At first, the frog thought it pleasant. The water was growing warmer, but it felt soothing.
> Soon, however, the warmth became heat, and the frog began to grow sluggish.
> Still, it did not leap out; it had grown used to the change.
>
> Little by little, the water grew hotter and hotter, until at last the poor frog's strength failed, and it could no longer move.
> It stayed in the pot until it was boiled alive.

What we learn is that when danger comes gradually, we may not perceive it until it is too late. This happens to us, over time, things happen. We collect baggage, preconceived notions, we become judgmental, and our vision becomes blurred, or, as Jesus put it, dulled.

That does not change the truth that the harvest is plentiful for those who have eyes to see it. The good news is that we have been given the very vision that the prophets longed to have. All that remains is for us to open our eyes and see what God is already doing.

> **He saw beyond the surface, knowing that transformation in each of us was not instant but a process of feeding, watering, pruning, and waiting.**

Through the green lens, Jesus was teaching that growth is possible when God's glorious Word takes root in the soil of a receptive heart. He saw beyond the surface, knowing that transformation in each of us was not instant but a process of feeding, watering, pruning, and waiting.

From Fisherman to Fisher Man - Peter

When Jesus first called Peter, he was an impulsive fisherman, often speaking before thinking and quick to act out of fear. We all know that Peter at one point denied Jesus three times. Yet Jesus never gave up on him. Through the green lens, He saw who Peter would become: a bold preacher, a shepherd of the church, a man transformed by grace.

On the day of Pentecost, it was Peter who stood before thousands and proclaimed the gospel with power, leading many to salvation. What an experience it must have been to watch the fisherman become the fisher of men.

That is the power of the green lens, Jesus sees not just who we are but who we are becoming.

From Murderer to Martyr - Paul

On the road to Damascus with one thought on his mind, to carry out the orders of the high priest, arrest the followers of "the Way", and persecute them as he had done on many occasions before, just like he had done when he approved of Stephen's execution in Acts 7. Yet Jesus never gave up on him. He met him where he was, on the road to Damascus, and blinded him so that he might see.

Later, Paul's healing represented the opening of his spiritual eyes to see Jesus as his Lord and Savior. After Paul's transformation, he became one of the greatest apostles in history. He traveled throughout the Roman Empire. He was the ultimate church planter. He wrote 13 letters to the church. He had the foundation for multiple key doctrines of the faith. He was also foundational at the Jerusalem Council in Acts 15 in paving the way for Gentiles, yes me and probably you as well, to worship alongside the Jews.

That is the power of the green lens, Jesus sees us not as that weak plant, but the powerhouse of the Oak that we may eventually become.

Transformation Takes Time

Christian growth is rarely immediate and takes time. The green lens reminds us that transformation is a process. We see that when Jesus compared the kingdom of God to a mustard seed

Mark 4:30-32 30 And he said, "With what can we compare the kingdom of God, or what parable shall we use for it? 31 It is like a grain of mustard seed, which, when sown on the ground, is the smallest of all the seeds on earth, 32 yet when it is sown it grows up and becomes larger than all the garden plants and puts out large branches, so that the birds of the air can make nests in its shade."

Take heart, because Jesus sees the tiniest of us as being able to become the foundation, the rocks of His ministry. Not because of what we are, but because of the transformation that He has in store for us. It is because He feeds us, it is because He provides us with the living water, it is because He gives us the sunlight to survive.

John 15:1-5 "I am the true vine, and my Father is the vinedresser. 2 Every branch in me that does not bear fruit he takes away, and every branch that does bear fruit he prunes, that it may bear more fruit. 3 Already you are clean because of the word that I have spoken to you. 4 Abide in me, and I in you. As the branch cannot bear fruit by itself, unless it abides in the vine, neither can you, unless you abide in me. 5 I am the vine; you are the branches. Whoever abides in me and I in him, he it is that bears much fruit, for apart from me you can do nothing.

Transformation takes time. The mustard seed did not become a tree in a single day. God already possesses perfect patience, but when we look through the green lens, we begin to share in that patience, both with ourselves and with others.

The Cross and New Life

Many people have a tendency to look upon the cross as the place where Jesus died for our sins, but the cross is not a place of death; it is a place where life begins.

Paul reminds us in 2 Corinthians 5:17 "Therefore, if anyone is in Christ, he is a new creation. The old has passed away; behold, the new has come."

The green lens sees every believer as a work in progress; redeemed, renewed, and living a life of sanctification that is only given by the Spirit of God.

Living Through the Green Lens

To see the world through the green lens is to understand that we are all a work in progress. God is not finished with us yet. He has compassion for His people, and the Bible promises that He will finish the work that He started.

> **Encourage growth** - remind people of who they are becoming, not just who they've been.
>
> Encouraging growth requires investing in others and stopping to see their potential. It's about seeing people

not just for who they are now, but for who they might become. This means taking time to offer words of encouragement and support that helps them also notice their potential. In order to do this, you have to get to know them so that you can invest in them.

Be patient - transformation is a process; give others the grace you desire for yourself.

Transformation for ourselves or others is a gradual process that takes time. Just as you want others to be patient with you as you grow, it is important to extend that same grace to others. Understand that everyone has a unique journey, which is why there are different parts to the body; each has a different purpose. Change doesn't happen overnight; being patient means offering support and understanding, even when progress may appear slow or when a setback occurs.

Invest in discipleship - growth requires nurturing through teaching, accountability, and love.

Investing in discipleship means committing to the growth and development of others through teaching, accountability, and love. This involves sharing your knowledge, experience, and most importantly, your time. It also means holding yourself and others accountable in a loving and constructive way. Discipleship is about building strong relationships that foster growth and transformation through Christ.

Celebrate the process - every step toward Christ is evidence of His transforming power.

Every step toward Christ should be first and foremost a testament to his transforming power. Celebrating the process means celebrating Christ with each and every step. It means rejoicing in both the small and large victories along the way. It is also about acknowledging that growth (sanctification) is a journey, not a sprint. There will be bumps in the road, but the journey is important. Encourage others to keep moving forward and remind them of where they came from.

Reflection Questions

1. Where have you seen the green lens of growth at work in your own life?
2. Who around you needs encouragement to keep growing in faith?
3. How can you begin to see others not just as they are today, but as Christ is shaping them to be?

Prayer:

Father, we pray that you allow us to see the world through the green lens of growth and transformation. Let us recognize the beauty in the process of becoming what you already know we will become. Let us see that this lens is the lens of your nurturing love and the new life that you have planned for us.

Give us the patience to trust in Your timing, to understand that transformation is a process, and give us strength as we go on this journey. Grant us Your grace as we grow and transform, and give us the ability to give that same grace to others. Help us to be encouragers and uplift others, allow us to be patient and kind. May we always find joy in the journey and to be thankful for the love that You have given to us.

In Christ's name we pray,

Amen

Living it out:

This week, put on the green lens of growth and transformation to see others and yourself differently. Set aside your critical nature that diminishes self-worth and see people as a beautiful work in progress.

Take some time to let someone close to you know that you can see the work that God is doing in their life. Take some time to notice the transformation. Be the encourager for them and let them know that you have noticed.

Use this space to write about the experience.

_____

_____

_____

_____

_____

_____

_____

_____

Chapter 6: The Black Lens of Reality and Sin

John 8:1-11 ¹ but Jesus went to the Mount of Olives. ² Early in the morning he came again to the temple. All the people came to him, and he sat down and taught them. ³ The scribes and the Pharisees brought a woman who had been caught in adultery, and placing her in the midst ⁴ they said to him, "Teacher, this woman has been caught in the act of adultery. ⁵ Now in the Law, Moses commanded us to stone such women. So what do you say?" ⁶ This they said to test him, that they might have some charge to bring against him. Jesus bent down and wrote with his finger on the ground. ⁷ And as they continued to ask him, he stood up and said to them, "Let him who is without sin among you be the first to

> throw a stone at her." [8] And once more he bent down and wrote on the ground. [9] But when they heard it, they went away one by one, beginning with the older ones, and Jesus was left alone with the woman standing before him. [10] Jesus stood up and said to her, "Woman, where are they? Has no one condemned you?" [11] She said, "No one, Lord." And Jesus said, "Neither do I condemn you; go, and from now on sin no more."
>
> Romans 3:23 for all have sinned and fall short of the glory of God,

---

Sin is deceptive; it hides in the darkness of the shadows. It lurks in the darkness of the night. Sin is the most comfortable in the absence of light, in the hidden places where the reality of truth is blinded. This blindness means that opening one's eyes reveals the true separation from God that sin brings with it. And that is, in no small words, painful.

Jesus didn't look away; He did not turn His head. Jesus looked at the world with eyes wide open, seeing both the darkness as well as the potential for light. Light is warmth, it is love, but sin flees from the light. He did not hide from the black lens; he saw through the black lens of reality and sin. Unlike us, He did not minimize it, He did not make excuses for it, He did not dress it up as if it were something that it was not.

> **He saw sin as it really is: destructive, deceptive, and enslaving.**

He saw sin as it really is: destructive, deceptive, and enslaving.

Out of all of the lenses, this lens is uncomfortable. As Christians, we prefer the brighter colors, the red of love, the blue of compassion, the gold of worth, the green of growth, yet the black lens is unavoidable. To see the world as Jesus saw it, we must recognize the depth of sin and the reality of its grip. Without this lens, the good news of the gospel is devalued to good advice, and the cross becomes arbitrary.

Sin Is Universal

We try to believe that we are above sin and that the rules of the black lens do not apply to us. We sometimes forget the grasp that sin had on our lives prior to Christ, but Paul captures the truth with devastating clarity:

Romans 3:23 "For all have sinned and fall short of the glory of God."

Such a short verse to have such a true and impactful meaning. It spares no one. Each and every person who has walked the earth has sinned; none are better than another. It is only by His grace that the Gold lens of divine worth is applied. The black lens removes the shadow and darkness, and then everything is revealed. Once revealed, there is no room for comparison or excuses. Sin is not limited to the obviously immoral, the criminals, or the scandalous. It is a shared condition of all humanity.

- **"All have sinned"** - not some, not most, not just the worst, but all.

- **"Fall short"** - we miss the mark, as hard as we might try, without His help, we will always come up short.

- **"The glory of God"** - the prize, His glory, but rightfully it can only be achieved through Christ.

This is the haunting black lens: the reality that no one can escape. It is who we are without Christ.

The Woman Caught in Adultery (John 8:1–11)

John 8 gives us a powerful example of how Jesus looked through the black lens of sin, not only at the woman caught in adultery but also at each person involved. His eyes were not narrowly focused; they saw everything.

John 8:1-11 but Jesus went to the Mount of Olives. 2 Early in the morning he came again to the temple. All the people came to him, and he sat down and taught them. 3 The scribes and the Pharisees brought a woman who had been caught in adultery, and placing her in the midst 4 they said to him, "Teacher, this woman has been caught in the act of adultery. 5 Now in the Law, Moses commanded us to stone such women. So what do you say?" 6 This they said to test him, that they might have some charge to bring against him. Jesus bent down and wrote with his finger on the ground. 7 And as they continued to ask him, he stood up and said to them, "Let him who is without sin among you be the first to throw a stone at her." 8 And once more he bent down and wrote on the ground. 9 But when they heard it, they went away one by one, beginning with the older ones, and Jesus was left alone with the woman standing before him. 10 Jesus stood up and said to her, "Woman, where are they? Has no one condemned you?" 11 She said, "No one, Lord." And Jesus said, "Neither do I condemn you; go, and from now on sin no more."

A group of religious leaders drug a woman into the temple courts in an attempt to trap Jesus. She had been caught in the very act of adultery. Parading her in front of their group, they were attempting to place Jesus in a difficult spot between the Law of Moses and the blue lens of brokenness and compassion. If He spared her, He would appear to dismiss the Law, but if He condemned her, He would contradict His message of mercy.

The scene was dripping with a vileness; it reeked of the shadows. Where was the man? Was he not guilty, deserving the same fate? Why the public outcry? Why the attempt to entrap? Was the sin important to the leaders, or was the lady just a pawn, a puzzle piece to accomplish another goal?

But Jesus' eyes were wide open, the image was clear, there was no distortion to the picture when He bent down and wrote in the dirt. What did He write that was so clear to those standing around Him? Then, in a powerful gesture, he stood and said:

> Not because she deserved it, she deserved the law of Moses, but what she received was the grace of Christ.

"Let him who is without sin among you be the first to throw a stone at her." (John 8:7)

One by one, the accusers left, until only Jesus and the woman remained. He asked her:

"Woman, where are they? Has no one condemned you?" She replied, "No one, Lord." And Jesus said, "Neither do I condemn you; go, and from now on sin no more." (John 8:10–11)

Neither do I condemn you, the only one who had the authority to forgive the sin, just set the woman free. Not because she deserved it, she deserved the law of Moses, but what she received was the grace of Christ.

Through the Black Lens

Notice how Jesus saw through the black lens in not one direction, in not two directions, but in a full 360 degrees:

1. **He saw the hypocrisy of the accusers -** Their self-righteousness blinded them from their own sin. They stood ready to condemn another, forgetting their own guilt. Through the black lens, Jesus exposed their reality; they were sinners too.

2. **He saw the woman's sin -** He did not deny her guilt. He didn't excuse it or call it a mistake. He

acknowledged the reality of her brokenness but responded with grace.

3. **He saw the people in the crowd** – Watching, waiting for Him to respond. They saw a King respond, looking through the Red Lens of love and sacrifice, and the Gold Lens of divine worth.

If the black lens stopped at exposing sin, then we would be guilty of the punishment of the law, which we are. But in looking through the black lens, Jesus doesn't stop at exposing sin; He prepares the heart for redemption.

The Nature of Sin

What exactly is sin? Too often, we reduce it to bad behavior, a list of wrong actions, maybe the Ten Commandments, but the black lens reveals a deeper reality.

Sin is rebellion - it is not just breaking rules but rejecting God's authority (Isaiah 53:6).

Sin is not merely about breaking a set of rules; it is fundamentally about rejecting God's authority. Isaiah 53:6 illustrates this by saying, "We all, like sheep, have gone astray, each of us has turned to our own way." Meaning that sin is a deliberate choice. A decision to choose our way over God's. It's an act of defiance against God's rightful rule over our lives, choosing self-will over divine will.

Sin is idolatry - worshiping created things more than the Creator (Romans 1:25).

Romans 1:25 explains that sin involves worshiping created things rather than the Creator. This means placing anything, whether it be material possessions, relationships, or our own desires, above God. Idolatry is about giving ultimate value and devotion to something other than God, which leads us away from Him and distorts our priorities and affections.

Sin is slavery - Jesus said, *"Everyone who practices sin is a slave to sin"* (John 8:34)

In John 8:34, Jesus says, "Everyone who practices sin is a slave to sin." This highlights the enslaving nature of sin. When we engage in sinful behaviors, we become bound by them, losing our freedom and becoming controlled by our desires and habits. Sin traps us in a cycle of behavior that we cannot break free from on our own, illustrating our need for the liberating power of Jesus.

Sin is death - its ultimate consequence is separation from God (Romans 6:23).

Romans 6:23 states, "For the wages of sin is death, but the gift of God is eternal life in Christ Jesus our Lord." This verse explains that the ultimate consequence of sin is death. This can mean both a physical death and the resulting afterlife without God, or a spiritual death in which we are also separated from God. Either way, sin creates a barrier between us and God. We see the seriousness of sin as not just about breaking rules, but an eternity without the presence of God.

The black lens reveals that sin has only one path that entangles, blinds, and leads to destruction. Sin, if left unchecked, will consume everything in its path, leaving behind total darkness.

Why We Avoid the Black Lens

Why do we resist looking through this lens? Because it forces us to confront realities we would rather avoid.

- It shatters our illusions of goodness.
- It silences our comparisons with others.
- It removes our excuses and self-justifications.

Looking through the black lens is humbling; it can and should bring us to our knees. It makes us confess alongside Isaiah:

"Woe is me! For I am lost; for I am a man of unclean lips, and I dwell in the midst of a people of unclean lips." (Isaiah 6:5)

The reality is that without looking through the Black Lens of Darkness, how can we truly appreciate the light?

Jesus and the Black Lens

The unique thing about Jesus is that He saw sin more clearly than anyone else, yet He never retreated from sinners. He lived among them. He ate with tax collectors, welcomed prostitutes, and touched the untouchable lepers. He looked at the world with perfect holiness, fully aware of its corruption, and yet He still chose to enter it.

> We have to pick up the black lens and not continue to push it away or set it aside. And when we pick it up, we must see differently. We can't continue to see sin and just dismiss it.

When He looked through the black lens, He did not see despair; He saw His mission. He came not to condemn the world but to save it (John 3:17).

We must change our perspective on how we look through the black lens. We have to pick up the black lens and not continue to push it away or set it aside. And when we pick it up, we must see differently. We can't continue to see sin and just dismiss it.

The Darkness in Us

The hardest part of the black lens is realizing that it, like all lenses, is a two-way lens. Sin is not only "out there" in the world; it is "in here," in our own hearts.

Paul wrestled with this in Romans 7:19 "For I do not do the good I want, but the evil I do not want is what I keep on doing."

Through the black lens, we recognize that the problem is not simply bad environments, poor influences, or unfortunate circumstances. The problem is that sins and darkness live within us. I am not sure who first stated it, and many attribute this quote to R.C. Sproul, but "We are not sinners because we sin; we sin because we are sinners."

This is the reality Jesus sees when He looks at humanity.

The Hope Beyond the Black Lens

If the chapter ended here, it would be unbearable. The punishment for sin is death. It is hard for us to imagine that. Someone once told me that the consequences of an action are based upon the value that we place upon the victim. For example, killing a mosquito has very few consequences. Running over an animal would have greater consequences. Killing a human, on the other hand, would have grave consequences. So, what would be the consequences for a sin against our savior?

David understood sin and relayed it to us in Psalm 51:4 Against you, you only, have I sinned and done what is evil in your sight, so that you may be justified in your words and blameless in your judgment.

The fact about sin is that our sin is a sin against the most holy of holies, and therefore, all sin is deserving of His judgment. But the black lens is not the final lens, although it is a necessary one. It strips away illusions so that we can receive grace.

When Jesus told the woman in John 8, *"Neither do I condemn you,"* He wasn't denying her guilt. He was pointing her toward the cross, where He would completely and totally bear her condemnation Himself.

Romans 3:23 is followed by Romans 3:24:

"...and are justified by his grace as a gift, through the redemption that is in Christ Jesus."

The black lens shows us our sin so that the red lens (sacrifice), blue lens (compassion), gold lens (worth), and green lens (transformation) can shine brighter.

Living Through the Black Lens

As followers of Jesus, how do we apply this lens today?

Be honest about sin. Don't excuse or minimize it in yourself or others.

Being honest about sin means acknowledging its presence and impact in our lives without making excuses or minimizing its seriousness. It's about recognizing that sin is a reality we all face and that it separates us from God. By being truthful about our own sins and the sins of others, we open the door for genuine repentance and transformation. This honesty is crucial because it allows us to confront sin head-on and seek God's forgiveness and grace.

Be humbled by sin. Sin can sometimes bring us to our knees, and that is ok.

Sin has a way of humbling us, reminding us of our human frailty and dependence on God's mercy. When we are brought to our knees by the weight of our sins, it is an opportunity to experience God's grace and forgiveness in a profound way. This humility is not about self-condemnation but about recognizing our need for God's help and the transformative power in our lives. We are lost without it. It's okay to feel the weight of our sins, but also to understand that it is through His grace

> **Like the Pharisees in John I, we must all drop our stones**

and power that the weight can be lifted.

Reject self-righteousness. Like the Pharisees in John 8, we must all drop our stones.

Self-righteousness is the belief that we are morally superior to others. In John 8, the Pharisees were quick to condemn the woman caught in adultery, but Jesus challenged them to examine their own hearts. Rejecting self-righteousness means recognizing that we are all sinners in need of God's grace. It involves dropping our stones of judgment and extending the same mercy and forgiveness that we have received from God.

Embrace confession. Sin loses its grip when it is brought into the light (1 John 1:9).

Confession is a powerful act that brings sin into the light, where it loses its grip on us. 1 John 1:9 tells us that if we confess our sins, God is faithful and just to forgive us and cleanse us from all unrighteousness. Embracing confession means being willing to admit our faults and seek God's forgiveness. It also involves creating a space for others to confess their sins without fear of judgment. Through confession, we experience the freedom and healing that comes from God's forgiveness.

Point to grace. The goal is not despair, it is not hopelessness, it is, however, redemption through Christ.

The ultimate goal of addressing sin is not despair or hopelessness but to point to the redemption available through Christ. God's grace is greater than any sin, and His love offers us a way out of the darkness. By pointing to grace, we remind ourselves and others that there is always hope and that God's mercy is available to all who seek it. This perspective shifts the focus from condemnation to the transformative power of God's love and grace.

When we see through the black lens, we realize that everyone is in the same condition, and everyone needs the same Savior.

Grace Illuminated by the Darkness

If anyone has purchased a diamond, they know that the jeweler will often display the diamond on a black velvet cloth because the darkness makes the gem shine brighter, and it sparkles more. In the same way, the black lens of sin makes the gospel gleam so much brighter.

Only when we acknowledge the reality of sin can we marvel at the reality of grace.

The woman in John 8 walked away no longer condemned by her past, but was saved by the mercy of Christ. We, too, can leave the shadows, forgiven and free, when we allow Jesus to deal with the darkness in us.

So, the black lens, though heavy, is not hopeless. It is through the darkness that we can open the door to light.

Reflection Questions:

1. Have you experienced a time when you wanted to hide from the black lens and just overlook sin in your life?
2. Did this chapter help you to progress through a tough issue that you had with the way that you viewed sin in your life or the life of someone close to you?
3. Do you often feel judged or justified by the black lens?

Prayer:

Father,

We understand that we have sin in our lives. Teach us to look through the black lens of reality and sin and see the depth of our brokenness and the areas where we have strayed away from Your path.

Please grant us forgiveness for our sins. Help us to see sin in our lives for what it truly is: destructive, deceptive, and enslaving. Give us the courage to be honest about sin in our lives and continue to shine the light of Your Spirit on us to see new sin as it enters. Thank you for your grace and mercy in forgiving our sin. Give us the strength to reject self-righteousness and extend the same forgiveness and compassion to others.

We are so thankful for the gift of grace and for the death, burial, and resurrection of Your son, Jesus, and that it is through His death that our sins were forgiven. Help us to live a redeemed and new life that was granted only through your grace.

In Christ's name we pray,

Amen

Living it out:

Use the black lens of reality and sin this week to first look at your own life. Be honest with yourself, is there something that you need to remove this week? After the introspective that you have used to look at your own life, have you applied the same grace to others around you? Are you carrying a stone in your hand that you are about to throw? Do you need to lay it aside? Is there work that you need to do in a relationship that would utilize the black lens? Take some time to lay down the stone and have a conversation with that person.

Write about the interaction you had below.

_____

_____

_____

_____

_____

_____

_____

_____

_____

Chapter 7: The White Lens of Purity and Restoration

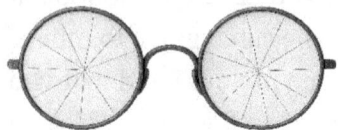

> *Isaiah 1:18 "Come now, let us reason together, says the Lord: though your sins are like scarlet, they shall be as white as snow; though they are red like crimson, they shall become like wool.*
>
> *Revelation 7:14 I said to him, "Sir, you know." And he said to me, "These are the ones coming out of the great tribulation. They have washed their robes and made them white in the blood of the Lamb.*

As we transition from the *black lens* to the *white lens*, we step into one of the great mysteries of the faith, one that Paul often spoke of in his letters to the Ephesians, Corinthians, and Timothy. It is the mystery of transformation, the divine exchange in which darkness gives way to light, and death gives way to life in Christ.

The *white lens* invites deep reflection. It is the color of light, holiness, and purity, an image of being made clean and whole before God. Yet we must understand that this purity is not something we can achieve on our own. No amount of effort can polish the stains of sin into holiness. The white lens is not a reflection of human perfection, but of divine grace shining through redeemed lives.

On our own, the white lens is unattainable. But through Christ, it becomes possible. His righteousness covers our imperfection; His light dispels our darkness. As Paul wrote, *"You were once darkness, but now you are light in the Lord"* (Ephesians 5:8). The mystery is that the same God who exposes the reality of sin through the black lens also provides the cleansing power that makes the white lens possible.

To look through the white lens, then, is to see the world and ourselves through the purity of Christ's finished work. It calls us to live as reflections of His holiness, not as those striving to earn it, but as those who have already been made new by His grace.

Throughout Scripture, white symbolizes righteousness and the purity of God Himself. As we read God's Word, there is always a barrier that resides between God and us; that barrier is sin. It is a barrier that we can't cross on our own, and it separates us from the holiness of God. The pathway to cross it is rather simplistic; it is the Blood of Jesus himself that allows us to join with the Father. To see that we must use the white lens of purity and restoration, God sees through that lens when He sees us purified and cleansed. He sees beyond the stains of our sin to the cleansing power of Jesus' sacrifice.

> **Where the black lens reveals the reality of sin, brokenness, and guilt, the white lens shows the other side of the story, restoration, forgiveness, and the wonderful miracle of being made new.**

Where the black lens reveals the reality of sin, brokenness, and guilt, the white lens shows the other side of the story, restoration, forgiveness, and the wonderful miracle of being made new. The white lens doesn't deny the stain; it shows how the blood of Jesus covers it and completely washes it away.

The Problem of Stains

Isaiah paints a vivid image of how sin stains us:

Isaiah 1:18 "Come now, let us reason together, says the Lord: though your sins are like scarlet, they shall be as white as snow; though they are red like crimson, they shall become like wool.

Sins are like scarlet and crimson colors that create deep, permanent stains that ordinary washing cannot remove. If you think about a grape wine stain on a white carpet or a mustard stain on a white shirt, scrubbing alone will not remove it. Going all the way back to ancient times in the bible, the Israelites would have known that scarlet and crimson dyes were nearly impossible to remove from fabric. People of that time would have clearly known that to remove stains, one of two things would have had to happen: a miracle, or the garment would have had to be replaced.

We live in a world full of stained souls. It's apparent that the stains and the lingering effect from the heavy burdens can appear to drip from our lives constantly, like a dripping faucet. The splash of each drop draws our attention back to our sin.

The church analogy of the iceberg is important; we only show people the top portion of the iceberg, and we block their access to our pain. How are you doing? Fine, Great. And to a blind church, that can be ok. People who smile in public while crying in private. Regret clings to the past like a scarlet dye that won't wash away. To the addict, or the victim, or the lost soul, these leave marks that we can't scrub off with works: good deeds, resolutions, or fresh starts. We carry things that labor to separate us from the love of the Creator, from the caring arms of Christ.

The truth is what Paul declared in Romans 3:23: "For all have sinned and fall short of the glory of God."

No one is unstained. Every robe is marked. Every heart has been soiled by selfishness, pride, or rebellion. The black lens of reality shows us this truth clearly. But the story doesn't end with a scarlet stain; it is only the beginning.

The Promise of Cleansing

Into this hopelessness, Isaiah speaks God's invitation: *"Though your sins are like scarlet, they shall be as white as snow."* Snow, freshly fallen, untouched, glistening under sunlight. It is pure, it is flawless. Have you ever seen a snowflake under a microscope? Google it; it is complex and amazing. God's promise to us is not just to simply cover the stain, but to completely remove it, to restore purity in a way that is impossible for us.

The vision in Revelation 7 echoes the same truth. John sees a multitude standing before the throne, clothed in **white robes**. Notice one thing, their robes were not white because they earned it, they were washed white in the blood of the Lamb.

This dichotomy is the heart of the gospel: the crimson blood that in a normal sense stains everything is what cleanses our soul. No human soap or ritual or penance can do this; it is only because of the cross that we are saved. How freeing is that message? I have always heard the saying "You can't good your way to God", and that is true. But you can accept the free gift that Jesus gave at the cross and the unbelievably powerful message: God's love is greater than any spot or blemish. It is through Him that we are made perfect.

Jesus and the White Lens

Jesus saw through the white lens. He didn't just see the sin through the black lens. He saw the cleansing that the white lens would offer.

- To the woman caught in adultery (John 8), He said, *"Neither do I condemn you; go, and from now on sin no more."* He saw the scarlet stains of the sin, but restored her anyway.

- To the lepers who were outcasts, He didn't retreat in fear; He brought healing and purity, restoring them fully.

- To Peter, who denied Him, He didn't turn His back but brought forgiveness and restoration. And then to show He was truly King, He put him in charge of shepherding His flock.

He knows we are not perfect, but He loves us anyway. Every step Jesus made, He saw not just stains but the possibility of white robes, restored, forgiven, renewed.

Purity Redefined

When we hear the word purity, we often think that, based on rules, it is something that we can attain on our own will. If we put on the right clothes or act the right way, we are good people, right?

But to be honest, purity is something that is unattainable by your works. No matter how hard we try, the bar is set too high. No matter how much we wash or scrub, the stain will not come out. Here is the miracle: it is not about being flawless by your own effort, it is about yielding yourself to the cleansing power of a mighty God.

- Purity is not the sinlessness that we achieve; it is the forgiveness we receive.
- Purity is not about keeping ourselves spotless; it is about being washed by the Lamb.
- Purity is not works; it is a gift of grace.

When Jesus restores us, He doesn't simply patch up our robes. He doesn't cover the spots, He makes them new. Our lives are not a testament of us; they are 100% a testament to Him.

Illustration: The Wedding Dress

Imagine for a moment a bride on her wedding day. She puts on a beautiful white dress, radiant and spotless, and as she is walking into the church, she stumbles and falls into a mud puddle. While trying to get up, a server trips carrying a platter filled with grape wine that drenches her. Then, to make matters worse, a bird flies over and guess what? I know this sounds impossibly unfortunate, but if we think about it, that is how our lives can sometimes look. No matter how hard the bride tries to clean the dress, the stain is not going to come out. The dress is ruined.

But what if there was a way to make the dress not only clean again but *whiter than it was before*? That is the miracle of the gospel.

The church is the *Bride of Christ* in Scripture. Jesus' sacrifice prepares us to be presented to Him "without spot or wrinkle... holy and blameless" (Ephesians 5:27). The white lens is the wedding lens; it shows us as beloved and restored, ready to meet the Bridegroom.

The Process of Restoration

Restoration is both **instant** and **ongoing**.

- **Instantly** - we are justified, declared clean by the finished work of Christ. The moment we trust in Him, our robes are instantly cleansed. We are white as snow in God's sight.

- **Ongoing** - we are sanctified, continually refined by the Spirit to live and practice being like Him. Each day, He restores, heals, and renews us.

The white lens does not promise that we will never stumble again. It promises that when we do, He is there to pick us up, brush off the dirt, clean us up, support us, care for us, watch over us, and most importantly, love us.

John 1:9 "If we confess our sins, he is faithful and just to forgive us our sins and to cleanse us from all unrighteousness."

The White Robes of Heaven

Revelation gives us a glimpse of our future: a great multitude from every nation, standing before the throne, clothed in white, holding palm branches, worshiping the Lamb.

This is not poetic; it is the promise. The white lens is not only about our present cleansing; it is about our eternal restoration. One day, all the stains of sin, all the scars of guilt, all the wrinkles of brokenness will be gone forever.

> **Heaven, or the church for that matter, is not filled with people who kept their robes spotless. It is filled with people who had their robes washed by the blood of the Lamb.**

Heaven, or the church for that matter, is not filled with people who kept their robes spotless. It is filled with people who had their robes washed by the blood of the Lamb.

Living Through the White Lens

To see the world through the white lens means:

Seeing ourselves as forgiven: refusing to live in perpetual guilt when Christ has already made us clean.

Seeing ourselves as forgiven means recognizing that Christ's sacrifice has cleansed us from our sins. This perspective encourages us to refuse to live in perpetual guilt, as we are made clean through His grace. It is about embracing the truth that our sins are washed away and we are no longer defined by our past mistakes. This understanding allows us to live in the freedom and joy that comes from knowing we are forgiven and loved by God.

Offering grace to others: looking past their stains to the restoration Jesus offers them.

Offering grace to others involves looking past their faults and seeing the potential for restoration that Jesus offers them. It means extending the same forgiveness and compassion that we have received from Christ. By doing so, we help others to experience the transformative power of God's grace and encourage them to move beyond their past and into a future filled with hope and renewal.

Pursuing holiness: not to earn purity, but to live out the purity we have already received.

Pursuing holiness is not about trying to earn purity through our own efforts, but about living out the purity that we have already received through Christ. It is a response to the grace we have been given, striving to reflect God's character in our daily lives. This pursuit is motivated by love and gratitude, rather than a desire to prove ourselves worthy. It is about allowing the Holy Spirit to work in us, transforming us to become more like Christ.

Walking in hope: knowing our future is a robe of dazzling white, a place before the throne.

Walking in hope means living with the assurance that our future is secure in Christ. We know that one day we will stand before the throne, clothed in robes of dazzling white, symbolizing our complete restoration and purity. This hope gives us the strength to persevere through challenges and trials, knowing that our ultimate destiny is with God. It reminds us that no matter what we face in this life, we have a glorious future awaiting us.

Reflection Questions

1. Where do you still see yourself through the scarlet stain of sin rather than the white lens of Christ's cleansing?
2. How can you remind yourself daily that your robe has already been washed white?
3. Who in your life needs you to see them through the white lens of restoration instead of the black lens of judgment?
4. What would it look like to live with the hope of Revelation 7, that your eternal robe is already secured?

Prayer:

Jesus,

You are the lamb who has taken away the sin of the world and invited me to live a life humbly for you. I stood before you, sinful and unclean, but you took away my shame and showed me your way. You washed away my unrighteousness, and even though my sins were like scarlet, you have given me a new robe to wear.

I pray that each and every day, you continue to wash me, to cleanse me in your mercy. My sins were purchased with Your precious blood; you have saved and restored me.

Teach me to walk each day in purity, seeing life through the white lens of your salvation. When I fall, pick me up gently and place me back on your path. Grant me the ability to shine my light so others see You through my actions, not because I am flawless, but because in my weakness, I was made whole by You.

Thank you, Jesus, for not turning away from my sin or ignoring it, but for restoring me so that one day I could stand before the throne.

In Your name I pray,

Amen

Living it out:

Take a moment to imagine yourself standing before God. In your own eyes, you see stains of guilt, regret, and failure. But then Jesus places a white robe around your shoulders. He looks at you, not as defiled, but as beloved. Not as stained, but as spotless. Not as broken, but as restored. Who in your life needs to be told the same thing this week? Who has been on your heart lately that you need to reach out to? Make that call.

Write about the interaction you had below.

_____

_____

_____

_____

_____

_____

_____

_____

_____

Chapter 8: The Purple Lens of Royal Identity and Calling

---

1 Peter 2:9 But you are a chosen race, a royal priesthood, a holy nation, a people for his own possession, that you may proclaim the excellencies of him who called you out of darkness into his marvelous light.

Revelation 5:10 and you have made them a kingdom and priests to our God, and they shall reign on the earth."

The Meaning of Purple

Purple is a mixture of red and blue light; it is not a primary color like violet. Our brain perceives purple as only one color, but in reality, it is two. If you recall, the red lens was of love and sacrifice, while the blue lens was for brokenness and compassion. Interestingly enough, we see purple when the red-sensitive and blue-sensitive cones in our eyes are stimulated at the same time, so purple is actually a color that our brain creates. In reality, the color purple only exists when the two lenses, the red lens of love and sacrifice, overlaps with the blue lens of brokenness and compassion.

Therefore, the purple lens rightly bonds those two colors together to create the lens of royal identity and calling. But this identity is only made possible not by anything that we did, but by everything that He gave.

In ancient history, purple dyes were expensive because they were created drop by drop from thousands of sea snails. Because of its rarity, purple was often a status symbol, especially in ancient Rome. Only emperors or high-ranking officials could legally wear certain shades of purple. Other shades of purple were so expensive that only the wealthy and powerful could afford the garments.

When Scripture uses purple, it is not just describing a shade; it is declaring identity. God commanded Moses to use purple in the tabernacle curtains and priestly garments (Exodus 26:1, Exodus 28:5-6). Soldiers mocked Jesus by dressing Him in a purple robe before His Crucifixion (Mark 15:17), symbolically affirming His kingship even in mockery. Lydia, the first convert in Europe (Acts 16:14), was a dealer of purple cloth, meaning she was likely a woman of influence and means.

The temple veil that separated the people from our Holy God was created of Blue, Scarlet (red), and Purple, which is an intriguing combination of colors since our red and blue cones in our eyes create the color purple.

The purple lens reveals how Jesus sees His people: not merely as sinners saved from judgment (black lens), not merely as cleansed and restored (white lens), but as sons and daughters of the King, brothers to Christ, called to live as royalty and priests in His kingdom, the purple lens.

Identity and Calling

There are two parts to this lens: identity (who we are) and calling (what we are meant to do).

- **Identity:** We are no longer orphans or outcasts; we are God's royal family.
- **Calling:** We are not passive heirs; we are active participants in His mission, serving as priests and reigning as representatives of His kingdom.

1 Peter 2:9 brings both together:

But you are a chosen race, a royal priesthood, a holy nation, a people for his own possession, that you may proclaim the excellencies of him who called you out of darkness into his marvelous light.

We are a chosen race (identity), a royal priesthood (identity), a holy nation (identity), and a people for His possession. Why? So that we may proclaim His excellencies (calling).

Revelation 5:10 echoes the same truth:

and you have made them a kingdom and priests to our God, and they shall reign on the earth.

Because of Jesus, His people have been turned into a kingdom and priests.

To look through the purple lens is to see ourselves and others not as common, or worthless, or powerless, but as children of God, entrusted with a divine assignment.

Jesus and the Purple Lens

Jesus Himself wore purple, but in a way filled with irony and pain. At His crucifixion, the Roman soldiers mocked Him by dressing Him in a purple robe and placing a crown of thorns on His head (Mark 15:17). They laughed at the idea that this beaten man could be a king.

What they mocked was, in fact, the truest reality. Jesus is the King of Kings. His purple robe, stained with His own blood, became the promise of our future. Through His death, burial, and resurrection, He secured royal identity for all who belong to Him.

When Jesus looked at people, He saw not just what they were but what they were called to be.

- He looked at fishermen and saw apostles.

- He looked at tax collectors and saw evangelists.
- He looked at women forgotten by society and saw witnesses to His resurrection.
- He looked at His church and saw a kingdom of saints.

Through the purple lens, Jesus sees beyond human limitation to divine destiny.

From Orphan to Heir

The enemy is the great liar, and one of his greatest lies is that: *"You don't belong. You are worthless. You have no identity."* He tries to beat you down, to call you unworthy, to steal your identity. If it were up to him, he would leave you orphaned, abandoned, purposeless. But the good news of the gospel tells a different story.

Paul writes in Romans 8:15-17:

"For you did not receive the spirit of slavery to fall back into fear, but you have received the Spirit of adoption as sons, by whom we cry, 'Abba! Father!' The Spirit himself bears witness with our spirit that we are children of God, and if children, then heirs—heirs of God and fellow heirs with Christ."

The purple lens gives an amazing pedigree to the orphaned spirit. Through the blood of Jesus Christ, we who were lost are adopted into the family. You are not just saved from sin, you are given a full birthright.

Royal Priesthood

What does it mean to be a "royal priesthood"?

- **Royal** - we share in Christ's authority as King. We represent His kingdom on earth.

- **Priesthood** - we have been invited into God's presence, offering prayers, interceding for others, and pointing the world to Christ.

In the Old Testament, the roles of king and priest were separate. But in Jesus, they come together. He is both King and High Priest. And through Him, we are given a crown and a robe, meaning every believer has authority and a place in the kingdom, not because of human status but because of divine calling.

A New Way of Seeing Others

When we look through the purple lens, we stop seeing ourselves and others as ordinary or insignificant. We see a royal identity and calling. If you are reading this and you are a follower of Jesus, then that means you have a royal identity.

- The teenager struggling with insecurity is not just a kid; he is a future priest in God's kingdom.

- The single mother working long hours is not just surviving; she is God's chosen daughter, carrying His image with dignity.

- The elderly person in a nursing home is not forgotten; she is part of the royal priesthood, destined to reign with Christ.

The purple lens teaches us to treat ourselves and others with honor, because we are royal.

Reigning with Christ

Revelation 5:10 promises: *"They shall reign on the earth."* This reign is not about worldly domination or political power. It is about spiritual authority, bringing God's rule of love, justice, and truth into every aspect of our lives.

We reign when:

We forgive instead of retaliate.

Forgiveness is a powerful act that breaks the cycle of retaliation and vengeance. When we choose to forgive, we are not condoning the wrong done to us, but rather releasing ourselves from the burden of anger and resentment. Forgiveness allows us to move forward with a clean heart, reflecting the grace that Jesus showed us. It is an act of strength and love, demonstrating that we are not bound by the actions of others but are guided by the principles of Christ.

We bring peace into conflict.

In a world filled with strife and discord, being a peacemaker is a profound way to reign. Bringing peace into conflict means actively seeking reconciliation and understanding, rather than fueling the flames of division. It involves listening, empathizing, and finding common ground. By embodying the peace of Christ, we can transform hostile environments and build bridges where there were once chasms that could not be crossed.

We live with integrity in a corrupt world.

Living with integrity means adhering to moral and ethical principles, even when it is difficult or unpopular. In a world where corruption and dishonesty are prevalent, maintaining integrity sets us apart as followers of Christ. It means being truthful, fair, and just in all our dealings, and not compromising our values for personal gain. Integrity builds trust and respect, and it is a testament to the transformative power of the gospel in our lives.

We declare the gospel in dark places.

Declaring the gospel in places of darkness means sharing the message of Christ's love and salvation in environments where it is least known or accepted. It involves stepping out of our comfort zones and being a light in the midst of spiritual darkness. This can be through words, actions, or simply living out our faith authentically. By doing so, we bring hope and truth to those who are lost and in need of the saving grace of Jesus.

Whether we know it or not, when we reign, we are a reflection of Christ's character.

Dignity in Daily Life

Royal identity is not just for grand moments; it shapes daily living.

- When you walk into your workplace, you carry yourself as an ambassador of the King.
- When you raise children, you are shaping future heirs of the kingdom.
- When you serve others in humility, you demonstrate true royalty.

Living through the purple lens means walking with quiet and humble dignity, knowing you are chosen, valued, and commissioned.

The Enemy's Attack on Identity

Satan knows the power of a royal identity, so he constantly attacks it. From the beginning, he tempted Adam and Eve with the lie that they were not enough. He tried to make Jesus doubt His identity in the wilderness: *"If you are the Son of God..."* (Matthew 4:3).

Today, he whispers lies of shame, worthlessness, and insignificance. But every time we choose to believe God's Word over the enemy's lies, we put on the purple robe of our true identity.

Living Through the Purple Lens

To embrace the purple lens, we must:

Receive our royal identity - believe we are chosen, not because of worthiness, but because of God's grace.

Receiving our royal identity means understanding that we are chosen by God, not because of anything we have done to earn it, but purely because of His grace. This identity is a gift, not a reward. It is about embracing the truth that we are children of the King, adopted into His family, and given a new status. This realization should fill us with gratitude and humility, knowing that our worth comes from God's love and grace, not from our own achievements.

Live out our calling - intercede for others, share the gospel, and serve in love.

Living out our calling involves taking on the role of a mediator between God and others. This means praying for others, sharing the message of the gospel, and serving those around us with love and compassion. We are called to be a bridge, bringing others closer to God through our actions and words. This calling is not just for a select few but for all believers, as we are all part of the royal priesthood.

Treat others with honor - recognizing their dignity as fellow heirs of Christ.

Treating others with honor means recognizing that every person is made in the image of God and is a fellow heir of Christ. This perspective changes how we interact with others, as we see them not just as ordinary individuals but as valuable and worthy of respect. It means showing kindness, respect, and love to everyone, regardless of their background or status. By honoring others, we reflect the love and grace that God has shown us.

Walk in authority - not timidly, but as representatives of the King.

Walking in authority means living with the confidence that comes from knowing we are representatives of the King. It is about stepping out in faith, knowing that we have been given authority by God to carry out His will on earth. This authority is not about power or control but about serving others and advancing God's kingdom. It means being bold in our faith, standing up for what is right, and making a positive impact in the world.

Reflection Questions

1. Do you see yourself as an orphan or as royalty in Christ?
2. How do you live differently knowing you are a child of God?
3. Who in your life needs you to see them through the purple lens and call out their God-given dignity?
4. What "territory" in your life (home, work, community) is God asking you to reign over with His love and truth?

Prayer:

Jesus,

You are the Alpha and the Omega, the beginning and the end, the lion and the lamb. You are worthy, and You reign as King over every kingdom. Yet in my sin and my lowest place, You called me to be your own, You adopted me into your royal family, You have given me the privilege to be called a child of God.

Today, I put on the purple lens and see myself as You see me, chosen, loved, redeemed, and set apart. I will renounce every lie that evil tries to tell me about my worth. Your blood has purchased my freedom. You have given me a crown and a robe.

Grant me the ability to see others through the same purple lens, not with pride, but with purpose. Let me love like you love. Give me boldness to approach them and tell them of their worth.

When I am tempted, don't allow me to shrink back from sharing Your gospel, but remind me of who I am. When I am tempted to boast, remind me who to boast about. When I am weary, remind me that the crown on my head is not a weight, but a promise.

Give me the strength to walk this way each and every day.

In Your name I pray,
Amen

Living it out:

Picture yourself standing before God's throne. A robe of purple is placed over your shoulders. A crown is set upon your head, not because of your achievements, but because of Christ's victory. You hear Him say: *"Welcome to the Kingdom, my chosen child."*

a) How do you feel?
b) Your neighbor, who never went to church, gave his life to Christ on his deathbed, is standing next to you and receives the same robe. Do you see them through the purple lens?
c) The town drunk or addict walks into your church and gives his life to Jesus? Are you able to remove the lens you are wearing and put on the purple lens?
d) Find someone this week who needs to hear it and tell them they are royalty.

Write about your experience

_____

_____

_____

_____

_____

_____

_____

Chapter 9: The Yellow Lens of Joy and Hope

Hebrews 12:2 looking to Jesus, the founder and perfecter of our faith, who for the joy that was set before him endured the cross, despising the shame, and is seated at the right hand of the throne of God.

John 16:20–22 Truly, truly, I say to you, you will weep and lament, but the world will rejoice. You will be sorrowful, but your sorrow will turn into joy. [21] When a woman is giving birth, she has sorrow because her hour has come, but when she has delivered the baby, she no longer remembers the anguish, for joy that a human being has been born into the world. [22] So also you have sorrow now, but I will see you again, and your

> *hearts will rejoice, and no one will take your joy from you.*

The Meaning of Yellow

Nothing can warm the soul like waking up on a summer morning, walking outside, and feeling the warmth of the sun as it beams down on your face from Heaven. Yellow is the color of sunlight; it is the color of laughter, warmth, energy, and hope. It represents what cannot be stolen, joy rooted not in circumstance, but in Christ.

The yellow lens is the lens of joy and hope. It does not deny sorrow, hardship, or suffering. Instead, it shines a light beyond them, revealing that joy is deeper than despair and hope is stronger than loss.

When Jesus looked through the yellow lens, He did not ignore the pain of the cross or the grief of His disciples. But He saw the *joy set before Him*

Hebrews 12:2 2 looking to Jesus, the founder and perfecter of our faith, who for the joy that was set before him endured the cross, despising the shame, and is seated at the right hand of the throne of God.

Scripture tells us that He looked past the cross. He saw resurrection beyond crucifixion, reunion beyond separation, victory beyond sorrow.

Joy Beyond the Cross

Hebrews 12:2 reminds us of something remarkable: Jesus endured the cross for the joy set before Him.

Think about that. Crucifixion was the most shameful, excruciating form of execution the Romans devised, and they were masters at creating painful ways to execute people. Yet Jesus faced it not with dread alone, but with hope and joy, because He was able to see past the cross. When He looked through the yellow lens.

- He saw the joy of redeeming His people.
- He saw the joy of reconciling us to the Father.
- He saw the joy of resurrection, triumphing over death.
- He saw the joy of eternal fellowship with His bride, the church.

The cross was the darkest moment in history, yet the irony of it is that it was endured with the brightest joy in mind. That one moment in time created a future of hope for those who would humble themselves to kneel at the cross.

Sorrow Turned Into Joy

John 16:20-22, 20 Truly, truly, I say to you, you will weep and lament, but the world will rejoice. You will be sorrowful, but your sorrow will turn into joy. 21 When a woman is giving birth, she has sorrow because her hour has come, but when she has delivered the baby, she no longer remembers the anguish, for joy that a human being has been born into the world. 22 So also you have sorrow now, but I will see you again, and your hearts will rejoice, and no one will take your joy from you.

Jesus prepared His disciples for the sorrow of His death. He compared their grief to a woman in labor: pain and anguish in the moment, but joy waiting for them like a long-lost friend on the other side.

Their sorrow and ours as well is real. It hurts. Many times, we feel trapped inside of it, struggling to escape, but unable to find a path out. Jesus didn't sugarcoat it, but He promised a path. He promised that their sorrow would turn into joy, and that this joy would be permanent: *"No one will take your joy from you."* The same promise is true for us. Our hope lies in that promise, and we should hold on to that hope with both hands.

The yellow lens doesn't deny the reality of sorrow; it acknowledges it fully. But it insists that sorrow is not the final word. The final word will be joy for those of us who believe.

Jesus and the Yellow Lens

Throughout His ministry, Jesus embodied this lens.

- He rejoiced in the Father's revelation to "little children" (Luke 10:21).
- He turned water into wine at a wedding feast; the first miracle, a symbol of joy.
- He ate and drank with sinners, accused of being too joyful in the company He kept.
- He promised His followers abundant life, overflowing joy, and eternal hope.

Even on the night He was betrayed, He spoke of joy (John 15:11):

"These things I have spoken to you, that my joy may be in you, and that your joy may be full."

The yellow lens was not absent in Gethsemane, nor on the cross. It was most brightly demonstrated there, because hope was anchored, not in what had happened, but in what lay ahead.

The Difference Between Happiness and Joy

To see through the yellow lens, we must distinguish between happiness and joy.

- **Happiness** is circumstantial; it rises and falls with what happens to us.
- **Joy** is rooted in Christ; it remains steady even when life crumbles.

Happiness is fragile; joy is indestructible. Happiness is fleeting, Joy is everlasting. Jesus did not promise us constant happiness, but He did promise us unshakable, unbreakable joy: *"No one will take your joy from you"* (John 16:22).

Hope and joy are two sides of the same coin. Hope looks forward in faith; joy is the expression of gladness in realizing that faith.

In our society, the words *joy* and *happiness* are often confused and used interchangeably, but Scripture paints a very different picture. Happiness is real and valuable, but it can be fleeting. It is fully circumstantial and can change quickly. Joy, however, is deeper, sturdier, and more enduring. It is foundational. Joy is not a fleeting mood; it is a posture of the heart anchored in Christ as the only foundation. Without this anchor, we are lost and will rely only on happiness, which leaves us unanchored, untethered, and unable to weather the storms of life.

Happiness depends on what happens to us. If life is going well, if we receive the promotion, if our relationship blossoms, if the diagnosis comes back clear, we feel happy. It is a feeling. But when those things shift, happiness can vanish as quickly as it arrived. It is fragile, easily stolen by bad news, disappointment, or even just a difficult day. In fact, Proverbs 14:13 reminds us that "even in laughter the heart may ache, and the end of joy may be grief." Human happiness, as good as it feels, cannot sustain us through the valleys of life.

Joy, however, does not stumble; it does not crumble when circumstances shift. Jesus Himself made the distinction in John 16:22 when He told His disciples, "So also you have sorrow now, but I will see you again, and your hearts will rejoice, and no one will take your joy from you." Notice that He did not promise them constant happiness. In fact, He broke the truth to them, they would weep, mourn, and be scattered. But He followed that with a joy that could not be taken away. Why? Because joy flows not from the temporary

Because joy flows not from the temporary feeling but from a deep-seated foundation that rests in His presence, His promises, and His power to restore the lost.

feeling but from a deep-seated foundation that rests in His presence, His promises, and His power to restore the lost.

The Apostle Paul lived this truth. By earthly standards, his life was full of setbacks: imprisonments, beatings, betrayals, shipwrecks, hunger, sleepless nights, and constant opposition. As a matter of fact, all of the disciples had setbacks, Joseph had setbacks, Abraham had setbacks, and Moses had setbacks. Setbacks were often seen as a part of living a life devoted to God. However, are they really setbacks at all, or are they the training grounds for our faith? Those patriarchs led by example; they did not base their lives on fleeting feelings; they anchored them in looking forward to what God had in store for them. Very few people would describe the life of Paul as happy, but Paul wrote to the Philippians, from a Roman jail cell, "Rejoice in the Lord always; again I will say, Rejoice" (Philippians 4:4). Notice where the rejoicing is rooted: *in the Lord*. If it had been rooted in his comfort, health, or freedom, Paul would have had reason to complain, not to rejoice. Paul was grounded in Christ; therefore, joy could flourish even in the bleakest places.

Someone once said to think of it this way: happiness is like the weather; it changes day to day, sometimes hour to hour. Joy is like the climate; it is the steady, underlying condition that defines the atmosphere of your life. Happiness is a smile that fades with the sunset; joy is a flame that burns even in the midnight darkness. Happiness is based on chance; joy is based on choice. Happiness comes from the outside in; joy flows from the inside out.

This is not to say happiness is bad. It is a good gift from God, but it has its place. There is nothing wrong with enjoying life, laughing with friends, or celebrating milestones, but happiness is a feeling, much like sadness, pain, and anger; they all have their place, and all have periods of time where we feel them. Scripture tells us to "eat, drink, and be glad" (Ecclesiastes 8:15), but Ecclesiastes 3 also tells us there is a time for everything. Feelings like happiness are not enough to sustain the soul. When storms come, when suffering presses in, when the bottom drops out, happiness is too weak to hold us. Joy is what carries us through.

Here is the paradox of the yellow lens: we can grieve and rejoice at the same time. We can hurt and still have hope. We can face loss and still find laughter. Paul describes it perfectly in 2 Corinthians 6:10: "sorrowful, yet always rejoicing." That is the testimony of joy; it coexists with pain because it is anchored in Christ, not circumstances. And when the world sees a believer walking through fire with joy still intact, it becomes one of the strongest witnesses to the reality of Jesus.

The Prisoner's Song

In 1944, Dietrich Bonhoeffer, a German pastor, was imprisoned for resisting Hitler's regime. Facing possible execution, he wrote letters to his family filled with remarkable joy and hope. In one of his last letters, he described Christmas in the prison camp, not with despair, but with gratitude, laughter, and songs of praise.

When fellow prisoners asked how he could be joyful in such darkness, Bonhoeffer explained: *"Our joy is in Christ, not in circumstances. The light shines in the darkness, and the darkness has not overcome it."*

Shortly after, he was executed. But his words still radiate yellow; joy and hope that could not be extinguished by death.

Paul in Prison

This story reminds us of the time that Paul was in prison. Paul's story in Acts 16 gives us one of the most striking pictures of joy and hope in the darkest circumstances.

16 As we were going to the place of prayer, we were met by a slave girl who had a spirit of divination and brought her owners much gain by fortune-telling. 17 She followed Paul and us, crying out, "These men are servants of the Most High God, who proclaim to you the way of salvation." 18 And this she kept doing for many days. Paul, having become greatly annoyed, turned and said to the spirit, "I command you in the name of Jesus Christ to come out of her." And it came out that very hour.

19 But when her owners saw that their hope of gain was gone, they seized Paul and Silas and dragged them into the marketplace before the rulers. 20 And when they had brought them to the magistrates, they said, "These men are Jews, and they are disturbing our city. 21 They advocate customs that are not lawful for us as Romans to accept or practice." 22 The crowd joined in attacking them, and the magistrates tore the garments off them and gave orders to beat them with rods. 23 And when they had inflicted many blows upon them, they threw them into prison, ordering the jailer to keep them safely. 24 Having received this order, he put them into the inner prison and fastened their feet in the stocks.

25 About midnight Paul and Silas were praying and singing hymns to God, and the prisoners were listening to them, 26 and suddenly there was a great earthquake, so that the foundations of the prison were shaken. And immediately all the doors were opened, and everyone's bonds were unfastened. 27 When the jailer woke and saw that the prison doors were open, he drew his sword and was about to kill himself, supposing that the prisoners had escaped. 28 But Paul cried with a loud voice, "Do not harm yourself, for we are all here." 29 And the jailer[e] called for lights and rushed in, and trembling with fear he fell down before Paul and Silas. 30 Then he brought them out and said, "Sirs, what must I do to be saved?" 31 And they said, "Believe in the Lord Jesus, and you will be saved, you and your household." 32 And they spoke the word of the Lord to him and to all who were in his house. 33 And he took them the same hour of the night and washed their wounds; and he was baptized at once, he and all his family. 34 Then he brought them up into his house and set food before them. And he rejoiced along with his entire household that he had believed in God.

Beaten, chained, and locked in the inner cell of a Philippian jail, Paul and Silas had every reason to collapse into despair. Their bodies were bruised, their future uncertain, and their obedience to Christ seemed to have brought them only pain. Yet at midnight, instead of cursing their fate or rehearsing their disappointments, they lifted their voices in prayer and song. Think about this for a moment: their wounds were still raw, their freedom had been stripped away, and they were surrounded by the stench and shadows of confinement. If they concentrated on the moment they were in, then all would have been lost. But they didn't, they focused on their faith and the promise of the future, and in that moment, they chose to sing. That choice was not based on feelings, because their feelings screamed otherwise. It was not based on circumstances, because their circumstances were bleak. It was rooted in a deeper reality, the joy and hope anchored in Christ, a joy no prison could steal. Paul once wrote to the Corinthians, "We are sorrowful, yet always rejoicing" (2 Corinthians 6:10), and here in Philippi, we see that statement embodied. Their worship was not an escape from pain; it was a declaration that Christ's victory was greater than chains, that hope was stronger than despair, and that joy was not a mood but a weapon. Notice also the effect: the other prisoners were listening. Their midnight hymns became a witness, testifying that there is a joy not bound by walls and a hope not silenced by suffering. Then came the earthquake, a divine revelation that broke chains and opened doors. To most, this would have been miracle enough, but God wasn't finished yet. You see, the point here was not freedom from circumstance, but to give freedom to those who didn't even know they were in chains.

This scene invites us into the very heart of the yellow lens: joy that radiates in the darkest nights, hope that sings before the morning comes. When we put on this lens, we too can find a song in our midnight hours. Our prisons may not be stone walls or iron chains; they may be seasons of waiting, disappointment, loss, or heartache. Yet the lesson remains: joy is not postponed until freedom comes; it is found in the presence of Christ who dwells with us in the cell.

To live through the yellow lens is to believe that our singing has power. Power to sustain in times of darkness, power to encourage the weary around us, and power to invite God to break down the walls that keep us prisoner and torment our midnight moments. Paul and Silas remind us that joy is not the absence of suffering but the presence of Jesus, and when we choose to lift our voice in praise, heaven itself leans in and the world opens its eyes to see.

How to Cultivate Joy When Happiness Fails

If happiness fades with changing circumstances, how then can we learn to live in lasting joy? Scripture points us toward practices that anchor us in Christ and open our hearts to the Spirit's fruit of joy (Galatians 5:22). Here are four ways to cultivate joy, especially when happiness feels out of reach:

1. Practice Gratitude Daily
Gratitude shifts our focus from what we lack to what we have received. Even in hard seasons, there are always gifts worth naming, breath in our lungs, the beauty of creation, the presence of Christ, the promise of eternity. Paul wrote

in 1 Thessalonians 5:16–18, "Rejoice always, pray continually, give thanks in all circumstances; for this is God's will for you in Christ Jesus." Notice he doesn't say give thanks *for* all circumstances, but *in* them. Keeping a gratitude journal or simply naming blessings at the end of each day trains the heart to see God's hand at work, even in difficulty. Gratitude becomes the soil where joy grows.

2. Sing and Worship Through the Storm

Paul and Silas sang in prison (Acts 16:25), not because their circumstances made them happy but because their hope in Christ gave them a reason to rejoice. Worship has a way of lifting our perspective from our pain to God's power. Singing truth over our sorrow reminds our souls who God is and what He has promised. You don't need a perfect voice, you just need a willing heart. Some of the deepest joy emerges when we lift our hands in worship in the very places where we feel most chained.

3. Stay Connected to Community

Joy multiplies when shared. Isolation is fertile ground for despair, but community is where hope is rekindled. Paul often described believers as his "joy and crown" (Philippians 4:1; 1 Thessalonians 2:19–20). Being with other Christians, whether in corporate worship, a small group, or simply honest conversation, reminds us we are not alone. When your own joy feels dim, let someone else's faith walk beside you. And when you are strong, walk beside others to lend them your joy. That's how the body of Christ works.

4. Fix Your Eyes on the Future Promise

Joy thrives when rooted in eternal hope. Hebrews 12:2 tells us that Jesus endured the cross "for the joy set before Him." His joy was anchored in the coming resurrection and the redemption of His people. Likewise, our joy deepens when we look beyond today's troubles to God's promised future: a day when He will wipe every tear, heal every wound, and make all things new (Revelation 21:4-5). Keeping heaven in view doesn't minimize present pain; it reframes it. Suffering becomes temporary, while joy is forever.

Hope Anchored in Resurrection

The resurrection is the foundation of the yellow lens. If Christ had not been raised, joy would be an illusion and hope a lie (1 Corinthians 15:14). But because He lives, we have living hope (1 Peter 1:3).

Psalm 30:5

- Hope says: *the grave is not the end.*
- Joy says: *death has lost its sting.*
- Hope says: *sorrow may last for the night.*
- Joy says: *joy comes with the morning*

The resurrection means every tear has an expiration date. Every grief will one day give way to everlasting joy.

Yellow in the Darkness

The yellow lens doesn't mean life is easy. It means joy and hope are present *in the midst of suffering.*

Paul and Silas sang hymns in prison (Acts 16:25). The early church rejoiced when counted worthy to suffer for Christ's name (Acts 5:41). James exhorts believers to *"count it all joy when you meet trials of various kinds"* (James 1:2).

Joy is not denial; it is defiance. It stares at the darkness and declares: "You do not win because Christ has already triumphed."

Living Through the Yellow Lens

To live with the yellow lens is to:

1. **Fix our eyes on Jesus** - looking to the joy set before Him, and the joy He promises us (Hebrews 12:2).
2. **Endure sorrow with hope** - knowing it will turn into joy (John 16:20–22).
3. **Rejoice in the present** - experiencing joy in Christ now, even in trials.
4. **Spread joy to others** - being bringers of hope in a world full of despair.

Reflection Questions

1. Where have you confused happiness with joy in your life?
2. How does Hebrews 12:2 challenge you to endure suffering with hope?
3. What sorrow are you facing today that God promises will one day turn into joy?

4. Who in your life needs you to share the yellow lens of joy and hope with them?

Prayer:

Jesus,

Life is full of struggles and hardships, let me tear away the grief and pain and replace it with the yellow lens of joy and happiness. Give me the strength and the courage to rejoice in the face of pain and agony. Let the walls that have entrapped me for so long be replaced by Your loving arms.

Let me see others around me through the same lens. Let me be able to share the story of the Gospel so that others will be able to increase their faith and their love for you. Let me put my faith in You, knowing that one day, You are going to wipe away the tears and the pain.

I am so thankful to know that I am your son (daughter) and that Your promise is true and everlasting. Thank You for the cross, and thank You for providing me with strength each and every day.

In Jesus' name,

Amen

Living it out:

Have you been struggling with hope, maybe stuck in a sorrowful moment in life? Would it be helpful if someone were to tell you that one day, that sorrow will be replaced with Joy? Find someone around you who may be struggling with the same things. You may be saying that it is a hard task, but don't let this excuse stop you. There is someone that you know who needs an encouraging word. Take the time to seek that person out and go have coffee, just sit and talk, before you leave, let them know of the promises in Hebrews 12:2 and John 16:22.

Write about that experience:

_____

_____

_____

_____

_____

_____

_____

_____

_____

Chapter 10: The Gray Lens of the In-Between

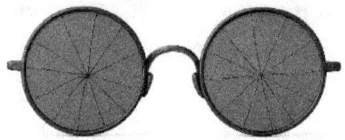

Luke 24:13–35 That very day two of them were going to a village named Emmaus, about seven miles from Jerusalem, ¹⁴ and they were talking with each other about all these things that had happened. ¹⁵ While they were talking and discussing together, Jesus himself drew near and went with them. ¹⁶ But their eyes were kept from recognizing him. ¹⁷ And he said to them, "What is this conversation that you are holding with each other as you walk?" And they stood still, looking sad. ¹⁸ Then one of them, named Cleopas, answered him, "Are you the only visitor to Jerusalem who does not know the things that have happened there in these days?" ¹⁹ And he said to them, "What things?" And they said to him,

"Concerning Jesus of Nazareth, a man who was a prophet mighty in deed and word before God and all the people, [20] and how our chief priests and rulers delivered him up to be condemned to death, and crucified him. [21] But we had hoped that he was the one to redeem Israel. Yes, and besides all this, it is now the third day since these things happened. [22] Moreover, some women of our company amazed us. They were at the tomb early in the morning, [23] and when they did not find his body, they came back saying that they had even seen a vision of angels, who said that he was alive. [24] Some of those who were with us went to the tomb and found it just as the women had said, but him they did not see." [25] And he said to them, "O foolish ones, and slow of heart to believe all that the prophets have spoken! [26] Was it not necessary that the Christ should suffer these things and enter into his glory?" [27] And beginning with Moses and all the Prophets, he interpreted to them in all the Scriptures the things concerning himself.

[28] So they drew near to the village to which they were going. He acted as if he

> were going farther, ²⁹ but they urged him strongly, saying, "Stay with us, for it is toward evening and the day is now far spent." So he went in to stay with them. ³⁰ When he was at table with them, he took the bread and blessed and broke it and gave it to them. ³¹ And their eyes were opened, and they recognized him. And he vanished from their sight. ³² They said to each other, "Did not our hearts burn within us while he talked to us on the road, while he opened to us the Scriptures?" ³³ And they rose that same hour and returned to Jerusalem. And they found the eleven and those who were with them gathered together, ³⁴ saying, "The Lord has risen indeed, and has appeared to Simon!" ³⁵ Then they told what had happened on the road, and how he was known to them in the breaking of the bread.

Living in the Grey

Life rarely skips from mountaintop to mountaintop. More often, we live in the valleys, in between peaks, on long roads that feel uncertain. There are seasons when God's presence feels distant, when His answers seem delayed, when our questions outnumber our answers. These are the *grey places* of life, not black with despair, not white with clarity, but shaded in ambiguity. We all face these struggles; we all walk this road.

The story about the road to Emmaus captures this reality. Two disciples walk the dirt road from Jerusalem to Emmaus in confusion. Prior to this walk, they had envisioned Jesus as the physical champion who would redeem Israel, but the cross appeared to have crushed that hope. They had heard of reports of an empty tomb, but their vision of the entire situation didn't yet make sense. They were caught between despair and faith, a road that we have all been on in life. They were caught between catastrophe, their world crumbling around them, and the vision of the full light of resurrection.

We all know this space well: the cancer test results not yet returned, the child away from home, the prayers not yet answered, the calling not yet revealed, the loved one estranged. Life in the grey is plagued by uncertainty. Yet, as we will see, it is in these very places that Jesus walks with us, often unseen, patiently guiding until our eyes are opened and our vision has been made clear.

The Nature of the Grey Seasons

When we talk about "grey seasons," we are not describing a rare or accidental experience of faith; we are describing the normal pattern of life with God. Scripture provides us with story after story of people who lived in the space of tension, of waiting, of uncertainty, of delay.

- **Abraham and Sarah (Genesis 15-21)**
  God promised Abraham that his descendants would outnumber the stars *Genesis 15:5 And he brought him outside and said, "Look toward heaven, and number the stars, if you are able to number them." Then he said to him, "So shall your offspring be."*

  Yet decades passed, and both Abraham and Sarah had grown old before Isaac was born. Each year tested their faith, especially as their bodies began to age and their circumstances looked impossible. The "in-between" stretched so long that Sarah laughed at the idea when she heard God's promise repeated (Genesis 18:12).

  12 So Sarah laughed to herself, saying, "After I am worn out, and my lord is old, shall I have pleasure?"

  But God was not late; He was working in His time, He was shaping their faith, showing that His promises depend not on our ability but on divine faithfulness.

- **Joseph (Genesis 39-41)**
  Joseph had dreams of greatness as a teenager, but instead of rising immediately to power, he was betrayed by his brothers and sold into slavery, falsely accused, and imprisoned. For over ten

years, Joseph lived in the grey space between vision and fulfillment. It would have been easy to believe God had forgotten him. Yet Scripture reminds us that the Lord did not leave Joseph; He was right there with him the entire time.

Genesis 39:2121 But the Lord was with Joseph and showed him steadfast love and gave him favor in the sight of the keeper of the prison.

The grey did not hinder God's plan. The grey did not divert God's love. The grey did not give authority to the devil that allowed him to creep in during the darkest hour and destroy or disillusion. It prepared Joseph for the future of leadership that God had planned.

- **Israel in the Wilderness (Exodus-Deuteronomy)** The Israelites were freed from Egypt in a mighty display of God's power, yet they didn't walk straight into the Promised Land. Instead, they spent 40 years wandering in the desert. Why? The wilderness was the grey in-between, a time of testing and training.

Deuteronomy 8:2 explains: 2 And you shall remember the whole way that the Lord your God has led you these forty years in the wilderness, that he might humble you, testing you to know what was in your heart, whether you would keep his commandments or not.

The delay was not about a punishment; it was about preparation.

- **David (1 Samuel)**
  David was anointed king as a young shepherd boy, but instead of immediately occupying the throne, he spent years running for his life from Saul. During this grey season, David didn't live a life eating grapes while servants were waiting on him; he spent his time hiding in the wilderness and in caves. During that time, he didn't just sit idly by; he wrote many of the psalms that we treasure today. The delay between anointing and crowning taught him dependence, humility, and resilience.

- **The Disciples (Luke 24)**
  Perhaps the most profound example of the grey was the three days between Jesus' crucifixion and the resurrection. On Friday, their hope was nailed to a cross. On Saturday, they lived in hiding, silence, and confusion. It was only on Sunday that the grey clouds were lifted and their joy returned with the empty tomb. The disciples' grey reminds us that even the darkest waiting is not the end; it is a process where resurrection is always waiting on the horizon.

The lesson we learn is that the grey lens is not an exception to a life of faith; it is the training ground that establishes our future. It is where trust is tested, where character is shaped, and where intimacy with God deepens.

The Grey Feels Heavy

Grey seasons are real, and they are never easy. The Bible does not sugarcoat the weight of waiting. It shows us men and women who wrestled with their questions, cried out in their pain, and struggled with doubt. These are not signs of failure; they show us glimpses of humanity.

Confusion

Luke 24:21-21 But we had hoped that he was the one to redeem Israel. Yes, and besides all this, it is now the third day since these things happened.

On the road to Emmaus, the disciples summed up their grief in three simple words: *"We had hoped."* That phrase resonates with anyone who has prayed for healing that didn't come, dreamed of reconciliation that never happened, or trusted for a breakthrough that seemed delayed. Time in the grey can be full of confusion.

Silence

Psalm 13:1-2

How long, O Lord? Will you forget me forever?
 How long will you hide your face from me?
2 How long must I take counsel in my soul
 and have sorrow in my heart all the day?
How long shall my enemy be exalted over me?

David cried, *"How long, O LORD? Will you forget me forever? How long will you hide your face from me?"* Silence can feel like abandonment, even though our hearts tell us that God is near; our minds can attempt to challenge that fact. One of the heaviest parts of the grey is the lack of clarity. Time in the grey can feel deathly silent.

Disappointment

Proverbs 13:12 - Hope deferred makes the heart sick, but a desire fulfilled is a tree of life.
Proverbs captures the ache of unmet expectations, the loneliness of depression, and the deep pain that can accompany waiting. Disappointment can weigh the soul down in the grey season. It draws in our attention, grasps onto it with both hands, and attempts to pull us down into sorrow. Time in the grey can be full of disappointment.

Restlessness

Psalm 42:3-5
My tears have been my food day and night, while they say to me all the day long, "Where is your God?" These things I remember, as I pour out my soul: how I would go with the throng and lead them in procession to the house of God with glad shouts and songs of praise, a multitude keeping festival. Why are you cast down, O my soul, and why are you in turmoil within me? Hope in God; for I shall again praise him, my salvation

Written by the sons of Korah, Psalm 42, we see the restless struggle between faith and despair. His tears have been his food day and night. We see the anguish that he is in.

The psalmist cries, *"Why are you cast down, O my soul, and why are you in turmoil within me? Hope in God."* His heart wants resolution, but God sometimes calls us to wait. Time in the grey can be packed with restlessness.

The lesson: The weight of the grey is not weakness; it is honest humanity. Scripture validates our struggle, showing us that even saints and psalmists wrestled in the grey area.

The Grey Is Where God Meets Us

But there is hope, we know deep down inside that the grey is where Jesus meets us. Here lies the paradox: while the grey feels like absence, it is the very place of God's presence.

- **Jacob's Ladder (Genesis 28:16)** After a night of fleeing and fear, Jacob declared, *"Surely the LORD is in this place, and I did not know it."* The grey often blinds us to God's presence, but He is closer than we realize.

- **Elijah's Cave (1 Kings 19:11-12)** Elijah, discouraged and despairing, expected God in the wind, earthquake, or fire. But the Lord came in a gentle whisper. Grey seasons tune our hearts to notice the whisper of the Savior.

- **Blurred Vision Luke 24:15** tells us: *"Jesus himself drew near and went with them."* The disciples did not recognize Him, but He was walking beside them the entire time. Their confusion didn't drive Him away; it drew Him closer.

- **Paul's Thorn (2 Corinthians 12:9)** Paul pleaded for God to remove his weakness, but the Lord replied, *"My grace is sufficient for you."* The grey may not remove the struggle, but it reveals God's sustaining grace.

The lesson: The grey does not signal abandonment; it should not be about loneliness, it is often the canvas on which Jesus paints. His hidden presence, revealed, teaching us to see with new eyes.

The Emmaus Road as Our Road

The journey to Emmaus is more than just a story of two discouraged disciples; it is a parable for every Christian walking through the fog of the in-between. It is about walking with our eyes shut, only to be revealed to the presence of God when they are opened.

In Luke 24:13-35

13 That very day two of them were going to a village named Emmaus, about seven miles[a] from Jerusalem, 14 and they were talking with each other about all these things that had happened. 15 While they were talking and discussing together, Jesus himself drew near and went with them. 16 But their eyes were kept from recognizing him. 17 And he said to them, "What is this conversation that you are holding with each other as you walk?" And they stood still, looking sad. 18 *Then one of them, named Cleopas, answered him, "Are you the only visitor to Jerusalem who does not know the things that have happened there in these days?"* 19 *And he said to them, "What things?" And they said to him, "Concerning Jesus of Nazareth, a man who was a prophet mighty in deed and word before God and all the people,* 20 *and how our chief priests and rulers delivered him up to be condemned to death, and crucified him.* 21 *But we had hoped that he was the one to redeem Israel. Yes, and besides all this, it is now the third day since these things happened.* 22 *Moreover, some women of our company amazed us. They were at the tomb early in the morning,* 23 *and when they did not find his body, they came back saying that they had even seen a vision of angels, who said that he was alive.* 24 *Some of those who were with us went to the tomb and found it just as the women had said, but him they did not see."* 25 *And he said to them, "O foolish ones, and slow of heart to believe all that the prophets have spoken!* 26 *Was it not necessary that the Christ should suffer these things and enter into his glory?"* 27 *And beginning with Moses and all the Prophets, he interpreted to them in all the Scriptures the things concerning himself.*

28 *So they drew near to the village to which they were going. He acted as if he were going farther,* 29 *but they urged him strongly, saying, "Stay with us, for it is toward evening and the day is now far spent." So he went in to stay with them.* 30 *When he was at table with them, he took the*

bread and blessed and broke it and gave it to them. 31 And their eyes were opened, and they recognized him. And he vanished from their sight. 32 They said to each other, "Did not our hearts burn within us while he talked to us on the road, while he opened to us the Scriptures?" 33 And they rose that same hour and returned to Jerusalem. And they found the eleven and those who were with them gathered together, 34 saying, "The Lord has risen indeed, and has appeared to Simon!" 35 Then they told what had happened on the road, and how he was known to them in the breaking of the bread.

Jesus shows us what it looks like to meet people in their uncertainty and lead them toward clarity. The five steps of this story serve as a model for how He deals with us in our grey seasons.

Step 1: Honest Conversations

> *"They were talking with each other about all these things that had happened. While they were talking and discussing together, Jesus himself drew near and went with them. But their eyes were kept from recognizing him. And he said to them, 'What is this conversation that you are holding with each other as you walk?'"*

The two disciples were not hiding their confusion; they were openly discussing their fear and confusion. They weren't pretending everything was fine. They were trying to make sense of what had just happened.

But notice what happens next: Jesus draws near and joins in the conversation. He doesn't immediately correct them, nor point out their faults; he poses a question. He asks them about their pain.

Application:
In the grey, God welcomes our honesty. We don't have to sanitize our prayers or dress them in religious language. The psalms are full of raw cries:

- *"How long, O LORD? Will you forget me forever?"* (Psalm 13:1)

- *"My God, my God, why have you forsaken me?"* (Psalm 22:1)

These aren't weak prayers; they are faith-filled prayers, because they are directed toward God. The road to restoration often begins with an honest conversation.

In Real Life:
Think of a grieving friend after a funeral. What brings comfort isn't someone rushing in with all the right answers, or the right verse of scripture, but someone willing to sit down and ask, "How are you holding up? Tell me what's on your heart." That is exactly what Jesus does here. He is a Savior who listens before He speaks.

Step 2: Understanding the Disappointment

Luke 24:18-21 "Then one of them, named Cleopas, answered him, 'Are you the only visitor to

> *Jerusalem who does not know the things that have happened there in these days?' And he said to them, 'What things?' And they said to him, 'Concerning Jesus of Nazareth, a man who was a prophet mighty in deed and word before God and all the people, and how our chief priests and rulers delivered him up to be condemned to death, and crucified him. But we had hoped that he was the one to redeem Israel.'"*

We hear one of the most heartbreaking phrases in Scripture: *"We had hoped..."*

These disciples had expectations; they had plans, and those plans had just taken an abrupt turn. They thought Jesus would overthrow Rome, establish Israel's kingdom, and bring political redemption. The death of Jesus shattered those dreams, for a moment. Now they walked heads down in distress.

Jesus, in His wisdom, gives them time to voice their pain; He doesn't cut them off, He doesn't interject with His plan. He doesn't tell them how they should feel. He listens, He is present.

Application:
In the grey, we must learn to understand the disappointment. We must admit:

- "I am struggling and had hoped for healing, but the pain lingers."

- "I am struggling and had hoped for reconciliation, but the relationship remains broken."

- "I am struggling and had hoped for a breakthrough, but the door still seems closed."

> **Understanding our disappointment doesn't drive God away; it draws Him near as we begin to work through the process.**

Understanding our disappointment doesn't drive God away; it draws Him near as we begin to work through the process. The disciples' confession became the doorway for Jesus to reveal Himself more fully.

In Real Life:

Again, at the loss of a loved one, we see a hurt spouse, hurt because they will never see their loved one again. The person understood that the Lord had a plan, but was hurt just the same. "I know I'm supposed to trust God, but I'm distraught because I no longer know the way forward." In that instance, do we see it pushing God away or inviting Him into the conversation? That is what Jesus wants from us: the courage to say, *"I had hoped..."*

Step 3: Receiving His Word

Luke 24:25-27 "And he said to them, 'O foolish ones, and slow of heart to believe all that the prophets have spoken! Was it not necessary that the

Christ should suffer these things and enter into his glory?' And beginning with Moses and all the Prophets, he interpreted to them in all the Scriptures the things concerning himself."

After listening, Jesus begins to teach. He opens the Scriptures, showing them how everything pointed to Himself. He reframes their pain and points to the future, God's plan.

31 And their eyes were opened, and they recognized him. And he vanished from their sight. 32 They said to each other, "Did not our hearts burn within us while he talked to us on the road, while he opened to us the Scriptures?"

Notice something crucial in these verses: before their **eyes** were opened, scripture affected their hearts. We need scripture to change the way that we see, and revelation begins with being hearers of the Word.

Application:
In the grey, the Word of God becomes our anchor. Feelings shift, circumstances change, but Scripture steadies us. It tells us:

- **God is faithful even when we don't see it**

    Lamentations 3:22-23
    22 The steadfast love of the Lord never ceases;
      his mercies never come to an end;

> *23 they are new every morning;*
> *great is your faithfulness.*

- **God works all things for good**

   Romans 8:28
   28 And we know that for those who love God all things work together for good, for those who are called according to his purpose.

- **God's promises never fail**

   2 Corinthians 1:20

   20 For all the promises of God find their Yes in him. That is why it is through him that we utter our Amen to God for his glory.

Even before clarity comes, the Word can cause our hearts to burn with hope.

In Real Life:
Consider someone waiting for test results, that could change their life forever. In that anxious week, they may not know the outcome, but they can cling to God's Word: *"Do not be afraid, for I am with you"* (Isaiah 41:10). The Word doesn't change the uncertainty, but it steadies the soul.

Step 4: Requesting His Presence

Luke 24:28-29 "So they drew near to the village to which they were going. He acted as if he were going farther, but they urged him strongly, saying, 'Stay with us, for it is toward evening and the day is now far spent.' So he went in to stay with them."

This is an amazing moment in scripture and shows Jesus' desire to be with us. Jesus, the

> **In the grey, Jesus often waits for the invitation so that He can begin healing our pain and revealing His plans.**

risen Lord, "acted as if He were going farther." He had places to be, but none were too important that He could not spend time with His followers. He waited for the invitation, and when they urged Him to stay, He accepted.

Application:
In the grey, Jesus often waits for the invitation so that He can begin healing our hearts and revealing His plans. He responds to our invitation. Our prayer can be as simple as: *"Lord I need you, please stay with me as I go through this."* His answer will always be yes.

Grey seasons are sustained not by clarity but by companionship.

In Real Life:
Think of being afraid of the dark as a child. What calms us is not necessarily understanding every question about what lurks in the shadows; it is about a parent coming and sitting in the room, spending time, and letting us know there is nothing to be afraid of. The same is true of our relationship with Christ; He may not answer all our "whys," but He gives of Himself freely and abundantly.

Step 5: Eyes Opened

> Luke 24:30-31 "When he was at table with them, he took the bread and blessed and broke it and gave it to them. And their eyes were opened, and they recognized him. And he vanished from their sight."

So why were their eyes opened?

It Was God's Timing

Earlier in the story, Luke notes that "their eyes were kept from recognizing him" (Luke 24:16). This suggests that their lack of recognition was a spiritual withholding. God chose the right moment to unveil Jesus' identity. Recognition of the identity of Christ was a work of grace then, as it also is in our lives today. We don't figure it out on our own; there isn't a magic prayer, God reveals it.

> Matthew 16:17, "flesh and blood has not revealed this to you, but my Father in heaven"

The Breaking of Bread

When Jesus broke bread, it mirrored the Last Supper (Luke 22:19), where He said, "Do this in remembrance of me." This act of hospitality and drawing close revealed the savior. It is sometimes in the simplest of times and the most humble of ways that Jesus reveals himself to us. It doesn't have to be at an amazing concert or spectacular event; it can be in the quietest of settings, where we hear the whisper of Jesus.

Scripture Prepared Their Hearts

Before their eyes were opened, Jesus explained the Scriptures to them (Luke 24:27). Their "hearts burned within them" (v. 32). In other words, the Word softened and prepared their hearts so they could finally see. Revelation always follows the delivered Word; God works through His Word first, then opens our spiritual sight.

Recognition in the Ordinary

Notice it wasn't a spectacular miracle or heavenly vision that opened their eyes; it was a simple act of breaking bread. This shows how Christ reveals Himself in ordinary, daily practices: meals, prayers, and community. Their eyes opened not on the road in debate, but at the table in fellowship.

The Pattern Cross → Promise → Resurrection → Communion

The sequence mirrors the whole Gospel story:

- Disappointment and confusion on the road (cross)

- Explanation of Scripture (promise)

- Their hearts burning, their eyes open (resurrection)

- Breaking bread (communion)

Their eyes opened when they invited Jesus closer.

Application:
The grey does not last forever. In His timing, Jesus will bring clarity. Often, it comes in ordinary moments, a verse that suddenly speaks, a prayer that brings peace, a meal with friends that reminds you of His presence. Keep strong in the faith and allow Christ to work in your life.

The Grey Leads to Burning Hearts

On the road to Emmaus, the disciples went from saying, *"We had hoped…"* to testifying, *"Did not our hearts burn within us while he talked to us on the road, while he opened to us the Scriptures?"* (Luke 24:32), because God revealed himself to them. Their eyes were opened, and they both saw and felt His presence.

The grey lens reminds us that Jesus meets us in every step of our uncertainty:

1. He invites honest conversations.
2. He allows us to name our disappointments.
3. He speaks through His Word.
4. He responds to our invitation.
5. He opens our eyes in His timing.

The grey does not mean God has abandoned us. It is often the very place where faith deepens, hearts burn, and Jesus is revealed.

> The grey does not mean God has abandoned us. It is often the very place where faith deepens, hearts burn, and Jesus is revealed.

Biblical Truths for the Grey

When the Word begins opening our eyes, we begin to see that there are some important biblical truths that we need to understand to move forward. These four truths will help guide you during moments of grey.

1. God Works in Delays

> *Habakkuk 2:3 "For the vision is yet for the appointed time; it hastens toward the goal and it will not fail. Though it tarry, wait for it; for it will certainly come, it will not delay."*

One of the hardest truths of the Christian journey is that God's timeline rarely matches ours. We live in a culture of instant gratification, microwave meals, two-day shipping, and on-demand entertainment. But God often works through delays.

God promised Abraham descendants as numerous as the stars (Genesis 15:5). Yet Abraham and Sarah waited 25 years before

Isaac was born. Joseph endured betrayal, slavery, and imprisonment for over a decade before God lifted him to power (Genesis 39-41). These stories remind us that waiting seasons are not wasted seasons.

Why does God work through delays?

- Waiting **shapes character**. Impatience is easy, but perseverance produces maturity

   Romans 5:3-5 Not only that, but we rejoice in our sufferings, knowing that suffering produces endurance, 4 and endurance produces character, and character produces hope, 5 and hope does not put us to shame, because God's love has been poured into our hearts through the Holy Spirit who has been given to us.

- Waiting **builds trust**. When our timeline crumbles, we learn to lean not on our understanding but on His faithfulness

   Proverbs 3:5-6
   5 Trust in the Lord with all your heart,
   *   and do not lean on your own understanding.*

6 In all your ways acknowledge him, and he will make straight your paths.

- Waiting **deepens dependence**. Delays strip us of the illusion of control and teach us to pray,

Matthew 6:11 "Give us this day our daily bread"

In Real Life:
Think of a seed planted in the ground. Nothing happens immediately. For weeks, perhaps months, nothing visible is seen. But what is happening beneath the soil is vital to the health of the plant. Beneath the soil, roots are forming and strengthening to support what will soon begin above the ground. Without that important foundation, the tree or plant will surely die. Delay is not death; it is preparation for life. The same is true of God's promises.

2. His Presence Is Closer Than We Know

Grey seasons often feel like abandonment. We cry out, but heaven seems silent. Yet Scripture reminds us that God's

Yet Scripture reminds us that God's presence is not measured by our feelings. He is near even when unseen or unfelt.

presence is not measured by our feelings. He is near even when unseen or unfelt.

The Emmaus story makes this beautifully clear. The disciples walked with Jesus for miles without recognizing Him (Luke 24:15-16). Their grief blinded them, but their blindness did not remove His presence. He was right beside them the whole time.

Why is this truth so vital?

- God's nearness **sustains us**. We may not feel Him, but His rod and staff comfort us.

  Psalm 23:4 Even though I walk through the valley of the shadow of death, I will fear no evil, for you are with me."

- God's presence **protects us**. Like Shadrach, Meshach, and Abednego in the fire, the Son of Man walks with us in the flames.

  Daniel 3:25 25 He answered and said, "But I see four men unbound, walking in the midst of the fire, and they are not hurt; and the appearance of the fourth is like a son of the gods."

- God's presence **guides us**. Even in uncertainty, He promises: "I will never leave you nor forsake you".

  Hebrews 13:5 5 Keep your life free from love of money, and be content with what you have, for he has said, "I will never leave you nor forsake you."

3. Faith Is Refined in the Grey

James 1:3-4 "You know that the testing of your faith produces perseverance. Let perseverance finish its work so that you may be mature and complete, not lacking anything."

Grey seasons aren't just delays; they are refining fires. They expose what we truly believe and whom we truly trust.

Israel discovered this in the wilderness. God provided manna daily, not enough for a month, not even enough for a week, but enough for each day (Exodus 16:4). Why? To teach them reliance, not reliance on the bread, their faith needed not to be placed in the bread but in the God who gave it.

How does the grey refine faith?

- It **purifies motives**. Are we seeking God for what He gives, or for who He is?

- It **strips illusions**. Comfort, wealth, and plans all fade, forcing us to cling to the unshakable
  Hebrews 12:27

  27 This phrase, "Yet once more," indicates the removal of things that are shaken—that is, things that have been made—in order that the things that cannot be shaken may remain.

- It **teaches endurance**. Like a muscle that strengthens under pressure, faith grows resilient when tested.

In Real Life:
Gold must pass through fire to have impurities burned away. Likewise, the grey is God's refining furnace. What emerges is not weaker faith, but purer faith, faith that can withstand storms.

4. The Grey Points to Greater Glory

The cross looked like the ultimate defeat. The disciples scattered, hope was buried, and darkness reigned. But three days later, resurrection reframed the story. What seemed like the end was actually the beginning.

Paul captures this paradox:
2 Corinthians 4:17 "For this light momentary affliction is preparing for us an eternal weight of glory beyond all comparison."

Why can we hope in the grey?

- Because resurrection proves that God is in charge of the final word, not death.

- Because suffering here points us to eternal glory there
  Romans 8:18 For I consider that the sufferings of this present time are not worth comparing with the glory that is to be revealed to us.

- Because one day, all waiting will end, and every tear will be wiped away
  Revelation 21:4 He will wipe away every tear from their eyes, and death shall be no more, neither shall there be mourning, nor crying, nor pain anymore, for the former things have passed away."

Living with Hope in the Grey

The Grey Lens doesn't deny pain; it acknowledges it while seeing through it. Delays, hidden presence, refining trials, and greater glory all remind us that God is at work in what feels like uncertainty.

The disciples on the road to Emmaus discovered this truth. They began the journey saying, *"We had hoped..."* but ended it saying, *"Did not our hearts burn within us?"* (Luke 24:32).

The same can be true for us. In the grey, hope is not lost; it is being reshaped.

Step 6: Living Through the Grey

How Do We Live Well in the In-Between?

The question isn't whether we will experience grey seasons, it's how we will live in them. Scripture doesn't promise a life without waiting, confusion, or uncertainty. Instead, it teaches us how to endure those seasons with faith. The disciples on the road to Emmaus show us a pattern. Here are six ways to walk well when the path is unclear.

Embrace Honesty: God Can Handle Our "We Had Hoped."

In Luke 24:21, the disciples confessed, *"We had hoped that he was the one to redeem Israel."* That statement drips with disappointment. Their hope was crushed, their expectations unmet. Yet Jesus did not rebuke them for saying it. He listened.

God is not threatened by our honesty. The psalms are filled with prayers that sound more like complaints than praise:

- *"How long, O LORD? Will you forget me forever?"* (Psalm 13:1)

- *"Why, O LORD, do you stand far away?"* (Psalm 10:1)

- *"My God, my God, why have you forsaken me?"* (Psalm 22:1)

Faith is not pretending everything is fine when it's not. Faith is bringing the raw truth of our pain before God. The road to Emmaus reminds us that honesty opens the door to encounter.

Practice: Try journaling your "we had hoped" prayers. Write down what you thought God would do but hasn't. Then leave space for Him to reshape those hopes. Keep the journal for a year and come back to fill in the blanks.

Stay in Community: The Disciples Walked Together, Not Alone.

Notice that the Emmaus story features *two* disciples walking together. They processed their grief in conversation, not in isolation. When Jesus appeared, He joined a community already in motion.

Isolation magnifies our loneliness and confusion. When we're alone, doubts echo louder, and despair feels heavier. But walking with others provides perspective, encouragement, and accountability. Ecclesiastes 4:9-10 reminds us: *"Two are better than one... For if they fall, one will lift up his fellow."*

Think also of Thomas after the resurrection. He missed Jesus' first appearance because he wasn't with the disciples (John 20:24). Community matters.

Practice: Who is walking with you in your grey season? Who are you walking with through their grey season? Seek out a trusted friend, pastor, or small group. If you feel isolated, ask God to provide a companion for the journey.

Anchor in Scripture: Keep the Word Close Even When Feelings Waver.

When the disciples expressed their confusion, Jesus responded by opening the Scriptures: *"Beginning with Moses and all the Prophets, he explained to them what was said in all the Scriptures concerning himself."* (Luke 24:27)

The Word of God is an anchor when the sea of emotions tosses us around. Feelings shift like waves, but Scripture remains steady. In grey seasons, you may not feel God's nearness, but His Word reminds you of His presence.

Psalm 119:105 declares: *"Your word is a lamp to my feet and a light to my path."* Notice, it is not a floodlight that illuminates that entire path in front of us for the next decade, but a lamp that provides enough light for the next step. That is often how God guides in uncertainty: one verse, one promise, one truth, one step, one day at a time.

> Notice, it is not a floodlight that illuminates that entire path in front of us for the next decade, but a lamp that provides enough light for the next step.

Practice: Choose one Scripture to hold onto daily in your grey season. Write it down and put a date beside it, memorize it, place it everywhere, repeat it in prayer until it becomes your anchor.

Practice Patience: God's Timing Is Different, but Never Late.

Jesus could have revealed Himself to the disciples immediately, but He chose to walk the entire road first. Why? Because the process was part of the revelation.

Habakkuk 2:3 teaches: *"Though it tarry, wait for it; it will surely come; it will not delay."* God's timing feels slow to us, but it is perfectly aligned with His purposes. Sarah laughed at the promise of a child in her old age, but Isaac arrived right on time. Lazarus died before Jesus arrived in Bethany, but the delay was so that resurrection glory could be revealed.

Patience in the grey is not passive. It is active trust, choosing to believe that God is working even when you cannot see it.

Practice: When impatience rises, add this to your prayer each day: "Lord, teach me to trust Your timing." Then reflect on a past moment where God's timing proved wiser than yours.

Invite His Presence: Pray, "Stay with Me, Lord."

As evening approached, the disciples urged Jesus: *"Stay with us, for it is nearly evening; the day is almost over."* (Luke 24:29). Jesus did not force Himself upon them. He responded to their invitation.

Grey seasons invite us into deeper prayer, not polished words, but simple ones. Sometimes the most powerful prayer we can pray is: *"Lord, stay with me."*

Revelation 3:20 echoes this truth: *"Behold, I stand at the door and knock. If anyone hears my voice and opens the door, I will come in…"* Jesus is near, but He waits to be asked.

> **Patience in the grey is not passive. It is active trust, choosing to believe that God is working even when you cannot see it.**

Practice: Begin and end your day with this prayer: "Jesus, stay with me in the grey." You may not feel an immediate shift, but

His presence will slowly become clearer.

Look for Burning Hearts: God Works Before We Recognize Him.

After their eyes were opened, the disciples said: *"Were not our hearts burning within us while he talked with us on the road and opened the Scriptures to us?"* (Luke 24:32). Even before recognition, Jesus was lighting a fire in their heart.

Sometimes in the grey, God is already at work, but we only see it in hindsight. That moment of peace in prayer, the verse that "came alive," the unexpected encouragement from a friend; these are burning heart moments. They signal His presence even before we recognize it.

Practice: At the end of each day, reflect: Where did I sense my heart stirred today? Write it down. Over time, these small embers will remind you that Jesus is near.

Living the Grey Well

The in-between seasons are hard, but they are holy. They invite honesty, community, Scripture, patience, prayer, and attentiveness. If we walk the road to Emmaus with these practices, we will discover that the grey is not wasted.

The disciples began the journey heavy with grief, but they ended it running back to Jerusalem with joy. That is the transformation the Grey Lens offers, not an escape from uncertainty, but the discovery that Jesus walks with us in it.

Encouragement for the Grey

When the grey feels overwhelming, remember:

- **Jesus walks with you** - even when unseen.
- **The Word burns within you** - even before clarity comes.
- **The table opens your eyes** - fellowship, communion, and simple acts reveal His presence.
- **The grey is not the end** - resurrection always follows crucifixion.

Reflection Questions:

1. Where in your life do you feel caught in the "in-between"?
2. What disappointments have you been honest with God about?
3. How has Scripture spoken to you in grey seasons?
4. Can you recall a moment when clarity suddenly came after a long wait?
5. How might God be shaping you right now through the waiting?
6. Where in your life are you currently in a "grey season" between promise and fulfillment, prayer and answer?
7. How does the Emmaus story encourage you to keep walking even when you don't see clearly?
8. What has the grey taught you about God's presence in ordinary places?

9. How can you support someone else who is walking through a foggy season right now?

Prayer:

Jesus,

I know that you are there in times of confusion, times of struggle, times of depression, times of grey. I beg that you will stay with me as I walk this road, never leave me nor forsake me, that is the promise that I will hold tightly to. I know that in times like these, you may be strengthening me, but it is tough.

I will hold steadfast to your promises, promises of strength, promises of delivery, and promises of your love and grace as I walk through this. I pray that you will send others to comfort me during this time, and that you will use it in some way for your glory. I pray that you will send me endless joy and comfort, knowing that you are my rock and my savior, and that I will build my foundation in your word. I know I am not the only one who is struggling, so I ask that you allow me and my actions to be a comfort to others.

Thank you for your loving arms,

Amen

Living it Out:

Living in the grey lens is tough not only for us, but for the people around us. Knowing that this session, because the grey is so difficult, we are breaking the grey into two parts, pick the part that most pertains to you.

Option 1:

You are walking in the grey lens and need to understand that Jesus is walking right beside you. Reaching out for help in times of grey is super difficult. Most of us desire to be in the yellow lens, not the grey, but for you, that is not the case. Dig deep and reach out to someone close to you, this is going to be tough, but necessary. Let them know that you have been walking in the grey and need support. Know this beforehand: some people want to help. Set up some time so that you can go meet with them and just talk.

Option 2:

Take a look around you, at your friends, acquaintances, and everyone that you come in contact with. More people are walking in the grey than you might imagine. Set up some time with them to just sit and talk, make it a weekly meeting or more frequently if necessary. Disciple them through in and through the grey. Use this chapter to help you navigate. Let them know that in seasons of in-between, Jesus is not absent, that He is with us on the road, patiently guiding us until the day the fog lifts and joy returns.

Write about your experience:

_____

_____

_____

_____

_____

_____

_____

_____

_____

_____

Chapter 11: The Multicolor Lens - The Full Spectrum of Grace

Revelation 7:9 After this I looked, and behold, a great multitude that no one could number, from every nation, from all tribes and peoples and languages, standing before the throne and before the Lamb, clothed in white robes, with palm branches in their hands,

Ephesians 3:10 so that through the church the manifold wisdom of God might now be made known to the rulers and authorities in the heavenly places.

Seeing the Full Spectrum

Light is only visible because of color. Have you ever watched as white light passes through a prism? I have a window in my house that allows the morning light to refract, and it creates an amazing rainbow of color on the opposite wall. Each color is magnificent on its own, but when the full spectrum is displayed, it is absolutely spectacular.

The same is true of God's grace. His grace is not single-sided; it is not one-dimensional. It is multicolored, multifaceted, and endless in beauty. Peter even uses the phrase "the varied grace of God" (1 Peter 4:10), reminding us that grace is not flat; it is a living spectrum. Many times, we only see one color through one lens. But sometimes we have the opportunity to see life through a multitude of colors.

The multicolor lens represents the fullness and completeness of Jesus' vision: the way He sees every group, every person, every story, every season, every lens we've explored, woven into one radiant whole.

Through this lens, we glimpse the harmony of God's plan: the love of the red lens, the compassion of the blue, the worth of the gold, the transformation of the green, the joy of the yellow, the identity of the purple, the purity of the white, the struggle of the grey, all converging into the full spectrum of grace.

This lens is cosmic in scope and deeply personal in application. We see it throughout the Bible as it spans eternity, yet it breaks itself down to the common areas to see how we treat our neighbor today.

The Biblical Vision of Multicolor Grace

1. The Multitude in Revelation 7:9

John's vision in Revelation 7:9-12 is a breathtaking image of different cultures and races united in worship:

9 After this I looked, and behold, a great multitude that no one could number, from every nation, from all tribes and peoples and languages, standing before the throne and before the Lamb, clothed in white robes, with palm branches in their hands, 10 and crying out with a loud voice, "Salvation belongs to our God who sits on the throne, and to the Lamb!" 11 And all the angels were standing around the throne and around the elders and the four living creatures, and they fell on their faces before the throne and worshiped God, 12 saying, "Amen! Blessing and glory and wisdom and thanksgiving and honor and power and might be to our God forever and ever! Amen."

- People from **every nation, tribe, people, and language**.
- Clothed in **white robes**, symbols of purity and redemption.
- Holding **palm branches**, symbols of victory and peace.
- Standing together before the Lamb.
- Elders, Angels, and creatures joining in

This is the full spectrum of God's promise to Abraham: *"in you all the families of the earth shall be blessed"* (Genesis 12:3).

The multicolor lens sees the church not as a monochrome crowd. Not as Jews or Gentiles, not as a single race, not as a single being, but as a tapestry of cultures and colors, each harmoniously reflecting the glory of God.

2. The Manifold Wisdom of God (Ephesians 3:10)

Paul writes that God's plan was to reveal His "manifold wisdom" through the church. The Greek word for *manifold* is *polupoikilos*, meaning "multifaceted, richly diverse, many-colored."

> **The church is meant to be the prism through which God's light refracts into the world. Not a single color of light that radiates, but a multicolored diamond that magnifies the darkness.**

In other words, God's wisdom is like a diamond that shines differently from every angle. His grace cannot be reduced to one color or expression; to do so would diminish the glory of God. To show the limitlessness of it, it must be displayed in countless ways through His people.

The church is meant to be the prism through which God's light refracts into the world. Not a single color of light that radiates, but a multicolored diamond that magnifies the darkness. Not a whisper of color but a shout or radiance that pierces the darkness. A mark that is so unmistakable that everyone sees its glory.

3. The Rainbow of God's Promise

From Genesis to Revelation, color is never random; it carries covenant significance. The first rainbow stretched across the sky after a storm that flooded the earth and gave a new beginning. In Genesis 9:13, God said, *"I have set my bow in the clouds, and it shall be a sign of the covenant between me and the earth."* The rainbow was not merely a natural phenomenon; it was divine artistry, God's declaration that judgment would never again consume the whole earth by flood. It was mercy painted across the heavens, a visual gospel long before the written one.

Every color of that rainbow reflects a different hue of His faithfulness, just as the colors of the lenses in this book. Together they proclaim that God's covenant of love spans the full spectrum of creation.

This same imagery returns in the final book of the Bible. In Revelation 4:3, John describes a vision of the throne of God: *"And he who sat there had the appearance of jasper and carnelian, and around the throne was a rainbow that had the appearance of an emerald."* The rainbow has moved from the clouds of judgment to the throne of glory. What once marked survival now marks salvation. The promise that once arched over a cleansed earth now encircles the King of kings.

The rainbow, therefore, becomes the thread that ties the first covenant to the final consummation. It reminds us that God's mercy has no end, that His grace doesn't fade after the storm but surrounds His people forever. The circle of light in Revelation shows that His promises are complete, unbroken, and eternal.

God's grace covers the world like that rainbow, shining through every culture, every story, and every redeemed heart. When His light shines through the prism of human experience, the result is a spectrum of grace. Each life reflects a different shade of His glory. Each culture refracts His mercy in its own way. And together, like the colors of the rainbow, the redeemed people of God display the beauty of His covenant faithfulness for all creation to see.

Living in the Spectrum of Grace

1. Beyond Monochrome Faith

> Too often, our vision of faith is monochrome, narrow, limited, and comfortable. We prefer people who look like us, worship like us, and think like us. Oftentimes, our churches are made up of those same people, people who look just like us. But Jesus sees life in its full spectrum. Throughout his time on earth, he lived, talked, and ate with people who were not like Him. People who were imperfect, people like us who needed a savior.
>
> The multicolor lens challenges us to expand our vision:

- To embrace believers from different cultures as brothers and sisters.
- To value individual and different spiritual gifts as essential to the body.
- To recognize that God's grace looks different in different lives.

As Paul writes
1 Corinthians 12:12, "For just as the body is one and has many members, and all the members of the body, though many, are one body, so it is with Christ."

2. The Harmony of our Differences

Think of a choir, each person singing at a different level. Many times, there are few, if any, solo singers in the choir. Singing alone, some may not sound as good as others. Each person has a unique sound, but together they create harmony. The more people you add, the better the choir can sound. The church should be the same. One note alone is beautiful, but the full composition requires every instrument.

The multicolor lens calls us to celebrate, not erase, differences. Unity is not uniformity; it is harmony.

3. Grace for Every Season

Not only does the multicolor lens speak to our cultural differences, but it also speaks to the rhythm of life's seasons. Just as the rainbow reveals God's promise through many hues, His grace reveals itself in many forms. The same sunlight of God's love refracts differently depending on the angle of our experience. In every season, there is a color of grace that meets us right where we are.

In **sorrow**, the **blue lens of compassion** reminds us that God draws near to the brokenhearted. His grace in grief is not loud but gentle, a steady presence that soothes the ache of loss. Like the deep blue of the sea, His compassion is vast and unsearchable. He doesn't rush us through our mourning; He sits beside us in it, turning tears into prayers and pain into intimacy with Him.

In **joy**, the **yellow lens of hope** glows bright. Grace here bursts forth like sunlight after rain, reminding us that celebration, too, is sacred. God's joy is not shallow happiness; it's the deep warmth of knowing that His promises are true and His goodness endures. Through the yellow lens, grace teaches us to rejoice in all seasons, to see even laughter as worship and gratitude as an act of faith.

In **sin**, the **black lens of reality** shows us grace's most sobering shade. It exposes what's hidden, not to shame us, but to set us free. The darkness of conviction becomes the backdrop for the brilliance of redemption. Grace here is truth unflinching, God's light piercing through our shadows. Through this lens, we see that grace does not ignore sin; it transforms sinners.

In **restoration**, the **white lens of purity** shines clean and new. It is grace that washes, renews, and rebuilds. The white lens reminds us that no stain is too deep for the blood of Christ. Where guilt once clouded our vision, grace now brings clarity. It is the light of forgiveness that makes all things new, restoring our identity and peace.

And in **calling**, the **purple lens of identity** reminds us that grace crowns us with purpose. Purple, the color of royalty, declares that we belong to the King. Through this lens, grace commissions us; it sends us into the world as ambassadors of the One who redeemed us. This grace gives us dignity, direction, and divine calling.

The spectrum of grace means that whatever season you find yourself in, whether grieving, rejoicing, repenting, rebuilding, or stepping into purpose, there is a color of God's grace waiting for you. His grace is

> **His grace is not one-dimensional; it is living and vibrant, shifting to meet every heart in every circumstance. Together, these colors form the full picture of His covenant love: a grace that covers every season, every soul, and every story.**

not one-dimensional; it is living and vibrant, shifting to meet every heart in every circumstance. Together, these colors form the full picture of His covenant love: a grace that covers every season, every soul, and every story.

Stories in the Spectrum

1. The Samaritan Woman (John 4)

The Samaritan woman lived under cultural, social, and moral shame. Yet Jesus met her at the well, offering living water. He didn't erase her story; He redeemed it. Through her, an entire village encountered the Messiah.

This is multicolor grace: it reaches across barriers, dignifies the overlooked, and turns outcasts into witnesses.

2. Cornelius the Centurion (Acts 10)

Cornelius was a Gentile soldier, far from Jewish identity. Yet God gave Peter a vision of clean and unclean animals, teaching him that the gospel was for all nations.

Peter declared, *"Truly I understand that God shows no partiality"* (Acts 10:34).

This is the multicolor lens: breaking down walls of prejudice, opening doors of grace to every person.

3. The Global Church

On any given Sunday, worship rises in countless languages and styles, drums in Africa, hymns in Europe, choruses in Asia, gospel choirs in America.

The beauty is not in sameness but in shared devotion. Each culture adds a color to the spectrum of worship around the throne.

Challenges to the Multicolor Lens

1. Prejudice and Division

One of the greatest threats to the church's witness is when it rejects the multicolored lens and falls into cultural, prejudiced, or denominational pride.

Paul confronted this in Galatians 3:28: *"There is neither Jew nor Greek, there is neither slave nor free, there is no male and female, for you are all one in Christ Jesus."*

The multicolor lens does not deny differences; it refuses to weaponize them.

> **The multicolor lens does not deny differences; it refuses to weaponize them.**

2. Comfort Zones

We naturally gravitate to what is familiar. The multicolor lens requires intentional steps to listen, learn, and love across differences.

3. The Temptation of Monochrome Gospel

Sometimes we present the gospel in one cultural form, forgetting that amazingly, the good news transcends cultural differences. The multicolor lens reminds us that Jesus can be worshiped in every tongue, in differing styles, and in varied traditions.

Practicing the Multicolor Lens

How can we live out this vision?

1. **Celebrate our differences in Worship:** Invite people, songs, prayers, and testimonies from different cultures.
2. **Seek Out Voices Beyond Your Own:** Read authors, listen to preachers, and learn from believers outside your tradition.
3. **Serve the Nations:** Support missions, welcome immigrants, and engage globally.
4. **Practice Grace in Everyday Life:** Extend kindness to people whose stories and struggles differ from yours.

The Spectrum and Eternity

Revelation shows us the end of the story: a multicolored multitude worshiping Jesus together. Until then, the church's role is to model that time each and every day. We are called to be a reflection of heaven's harmony, a living prism of God's grace.

Paul says in Ephesians 3:21: *"to him be glory in the church and in Christ Jesus throughout all generations, forever and ever. Amen."*

The multicolor lens invites us to live now in light of eternity, to see every person, every culture, every color of grace, as part of God's radiant plan.

Reflection Questions:

1. How do you naturally see faith: monochrome or multicolor?
2. What differences have you struggled to embrace in the body of Christ?
3. How might you begin practicing the multicolor lens in your community?
4. In what "color" of grace are you currently living (joy, sorrow, transformation, hope)?
5. How does Revelation 7:9 inspire your vision of the church today?

Prayer:

Father,

The multicolored lens teaches us that we are all different, but we all serve the same God. You are good, You are gracious, and You are perfect in every way. Help me to join in and worship with others, learn from others, and see that the Church is not bound by four walls. It is a labyrinth of cultures and races all worshiping Your glory. Your Church is the wonderful experience of differences, where all worship One true God. Seeing through the multicolored lens is seeing that your Son showed grace to both the Jews and the Gentiles. It is seeing that churches around the world all worship You, sometimes differently, but we all turn to the one true and singular Gospel.

Let me open my eyes to see the value of others, to see the wonderful and amazing people that you have created. To allow me to always see the good in others, to see that we were all created in your wonderful and amazing image. Let me understand that You poured Your Spirit into all races, all types of people, all cultures, and that Your Spirit allows us to be unique but to always put Your Gospel and Your instructions first in our lives. Let us see the wonder in your creation each and every day.

Amen

Living it out:

Imagine standing before the throne of God. All around you are people from every nation, tribe, and tongue. The colors of their cultures blend together in worship. The songs rise in harmony, different yet united. The light of God refracts through the Lamb and fills the heavens with radiant beauty. Is your current worship a reflection of this?

This week, find someone from a different race or a different culture and open up to them about the Gospel. Share with them, invite them to lunch, and just talk about Jesus. Use the space below to write about the encounter. Talk about the similarities and the differences that you found. How was the experience? Did it leave you wanting to do it again?

Write about your experience:

_____

_____

_____

_____

_____

_____

Chapter 12: Conclusion - Seeing through His Eyes

> *Ephesians 1:18 I pray that the eyes of your heart may be enlightened in order that you may know the hope to which he has called you, the riches of his glorious inheritance in his holy people,*

We began by putting on lens after lens, red for love, blue for compassion, gold for divine worth, green for transformation, white for purity, purple for royal identity, yellow for joy, grey for the in-between, and multicolor for the fullness of grace. Each lens taught us something about how Jesus sees:

- The **Red Lens** showed us a Savior whose love is costly and sacrificial, whose blood bought our freedom.
- The **Blue Lens** showed us a Christ who weeps with the broken and is moved with compassion.

- The **Gold Lens** reminded us that every person has infinite value — stamped with God's image and worthy of redemption.

- The **Green Lens** gave us hope for growth, reminding us that no one is ever too far gone for transformation.

- The **White Lens** assured us that Jesus can wash away every stain and restore us to intimacy with God.

- The **Purple Lens** invited us to step into our royal identity as sons and daughters, priests and co-heirs with Christ.

- The **Yellow Lens** called us to live with joy and hope, even in sorrow, fixing our eyes on the joy set before us.

- The **Grey Lens** taught us that Jesus walks with us in the in-between, even when we cannot see clearly.

- And the **Multicolor Lens** reminded us that grace is for *all nations, all tribes, all tongues*, that the kingdom of God is a breathtaking mosaic of redeemed humanity.

But the purpose of these lenses was never just to look at them; it wasn't to sit back and gaze at their beauty; it was to put them on daily and to *see through them.* To see through His eyes.

The Gift of Spiritual Sight

When Jesus healed blind Bartimaeus (Mark 10:46-52), it wasn't just a physical miracle; it was a sign of what He came to do for all humanity: to restore our sight. To fix our brokenness. As we saw in the first two chapters, our vision is impaired. Spiritual blindness keeps us from seeing the kingdom of God (John 3:3). Sin clouds our vision. Pain distorts it. Pride blinds us to the needs around us. And our baggage of life that we each carry causes us to see the world, those around us, and ourselves through a distorted lens.

But when we allow Jesus to touch our eyes, we begin to see:

- We see people as more than problems or projects, more than interruptions; we see them as beloved children of God.
- We see our enemies as image-bearers who need grace, not judgment.
- We see our own story not as a collection of failures, but as a testimony of Christ and His redemptive love for us.
- We see suffering not as meaningless, but as a place where God is still working.

Paul writes in 2 Corinthians 3:18,

"And we all, with unveiled face, beholding the glory of the Lord, are being transformed into the same image from one

degree of glory to another. For this comes from the Lord who is the Spirit."

Seeing Jesus transforms us, and as we are transformed, we begin to reflect Him to the world.

Living With His Eyes Open

This is where the book becomes a calling, a challenge to you. Seeing through His eyes is not just an inward experience; it is an outward way of living.

- **Through His Eyes, We Love Boldly.** The red lens sends us into a world desperate for love, willing to lay down our lives for others.

- **Through His Eyes, We Show Compassion.** The blue lens makes us attentive to the suffering of neighbors, strangers, and even enemies.

- **Through His Eyes, We Call Out Value.** The gold lens moves us to affirm the worth of the overlooked and marginalized.

- **Through His Eyes, We Believe in Growth.** The green lens helps us disciple others with patience, knowing God isn't finished with them yet.

- **Through His Eyes, We Pursue Holiness.** The white lens calls us to walk in purity, not out of fear but out of love for the One who washed us.

- **Through His Eyes, We Walk as Sons and Daughters.** The purple lens helps us stand tall in our identity, living as ambassadors of His kingdom.

- **Through His Eyes, We Radiate Hope.** The yellow lens makes us people of joy, holding light in dark places.

- **Through His Eyes, We Persevere.** The grey lens reminds us to keep walking, even when life feels uncertain.

- **Through His Eyes, We Celebrate Our Differences.** The multicolor lens inspires us to join the global mission of God, proclaiming His glory to every tribe and tongue.

This is what happens when the eyes of your heart are enlightened: life becomes a mission.

A Sending Call

I hope that you understand now that reading this book is not the end. It is the beginning of a new way of seeing. You now have a choice: to put these new lenses down and return to old ways of looking at the world, or to keep them on and let them shape every moment.

- Will you choose love when the world chooses fear?
- Will you choose compassion when the world chooses indifference?
- Will you see the broken as beautiful, the sinner as redeemable, the waiting season as holy?
- Will you live as though Jesus is near, because He is?

Your family needs you to see through His eyes. Your workplace needs you to see through His eyes. Your neighborhood, your church, your city, your generation, all are waiting for someone who will carry the vision of Jesus into the world.

A Vision of the End

John gives us a glimpse of the final fulfillment of this vision in Revelation 22:4: *"They will see his face, and his name will be on their foreheads."* One day, we won't just see through His eyes; we will see Him face to face. The lenses will no longer be needed, because our sight will be made complete. Every tear will be wiped away, every shadow gone, every question answered.

> One day, we won't just see through His eyes; we will see Him face to face. The lenses will no longer be needed, because our sight will be made complete.

Until that day, we walk by faith, not by sight, but with hearts enlightened, we see enough to take the next step.

Reflection Questions:

1. Which path did you take? Did you put the lenses on or take them off?
2. How often do you think you will have to make the decision above?
3. If you choose to put them on daily, how do you think the rest of your life will change?

Living it out:

Today, go to the store and buy a simple pair of glasses, on one lens tape a blue cellophane patch, on the other put red (you can actually choose any color from above). Set those glasses on a table, for conversation or just to remind yourself each and every day of the choice that you have made.

Now go out and live your life for Christ. Go out and see the world for the first time, through your new eyes.

A Closing Prayer

Jesus,
Open the eyes of my heart.
Let me see the world as You see it.
Let me see people with compassion,
myself with grace,
my future with hope,
and my calling with courage.

Forgive me for the times I have been blind
blind to the hurting,
blind to Your presence,
blind to my own need for You.

Touch my eyes again, Lord,
that I may see.
Let every lens I have learned become
a permanent part of my vision,
so that everywhere I go,
I carry Your perspective.

Until the day I see You face to face,
keep me faithful,
keep me focused,
and keep me looking through Your eyes.

Amen.

www.ingramcontent.com/pod-product-compliance
Lightning Source LLC
LaVergne TN
LVHW051831080426
835512LV00018B/2824